TAMPA BAY LIGHTNING:
2004 STANLEY CUP CHAMPIONS

St. Petersburg Times
sptimes.com • tampabay.com

Sports Publishing L.L.C.
www.sportspublishingllc.com

Publisher
Peter L. Bannon

Senior Managing Editors
Joseph J. Bannon Jr. and Susan M. Moyer

Coordinating Editor
Noah A. Amstadter

Developmental Editors
Elisa Bock Laird and Regina D. Sabbia

Photo Editor
Erin Linden-Levy

Art Director
K. Jeffrey Higgerson

Copy Editor
Cynthia L. McNew

Book Design, Book Layout
Jim Henehan

Cover Design
Dustin Hubbart

Imaging
Kenneth J. O'Brien
Dustin Hubbart
K. Jeffrey Higgerson

St. Petersburg Times

Editor, Chairman and CEO
Paul C. Tash

Executive Vice President
Marty Petty

Managing Editor and Vice President
Neil Brown

Managing Editor/Tampa
Neville Green

Assistant Managing Editor/Sports
Jack Sheppard

Assistant Managing Editor/Photography
Sue Morrow

Assistant Managing Editor/Presentation
Patty Cox

Softcover ISBN: 1-58261-554-3
Hardcover ISBN: 1-58261-914-X

Front Cover Photo: Dan McDuffie/St. Petersburg Times
Back Cover Art: Dirk Shadd/St. Petersburg Times

Contents

The bench clears and the crowd goes wild as the Lightning win their first-ever Stanley Cup. DIRK SHADD/ST. PETERSBURG TIMES

Editor's Note

Sunshine and ice aren't always a good mix.

But the Sunshine State and ice hockey have become a winning combination. And Florida's Best Newspaper has chronicled the transformation.

With the Stanley Cup safely in its new home, Tampa Bay has become its own version of Hockeytown. No, not everyone knows a check from a Czech. Some still confuse a power play with a Lightning strike. But make no mistake, hockey has captured its place at the top of Tampa Bay.

The Lightning's 12 seasons have been blunderful as Tampa Bay grew from an area where security went on alert when someone threw a hat on the ice to one where the NHL playoff attendance mark was set twice. We once saw a woman in goal and now understand how two months of playoffs can take their toll.

It all was preparation for this season in the sun. From Coach John Tortorella's challenging training camp, through the artistry of Martin St. Louis' magical season to the resurgence of Nikolai Khabibulin in the playoffs the *St. Petersburg Times'* team of journalists has brought you outstanding coverage. Now, through the words of beat writer Damian Cristodero and his colleagues and the great images from a photo team led by Dirk Shadd, we invite you to relive the memories.

But don't sweat the details. After all, the Stanley Cup has a new home. And it's Tampa Bay.

The Editors

STEFANIE BOYAR/ST. PETERSBURG TIMES

10 QUESTIONS ENTERING CAMP

DAMIAN CRISTODERO

You would think after such a successful season there would be fewer questions entering camp. Indulge us. These little dramas will make preseason much more fun.

1. Will Nikolai Khabibulin regain world-class form?

The goalie's reputation took a hit last season and he has a hungry backup in John Grahame itching for playing time. Those are great motivations. Khabibulin has risen impressively to most challenges. Remember his first game for the Lightning after being acquired from the Coyotes, his performance in the 2002 All-Star Game and in Game 6 of the East quarterfinals? Tampa Bay hopes he will rise again.

2. Can Cory Stillman replace Vinny Prospal?

Does he have to? The left wings play different styles and have different strengths. The bottom line will be Stillman's production and how he helps the production of his linemates. It is assumed Stillman will start on Vinny Lecavalier's line. The center flourished thanks to Prospal's pinpoint passes. Stillman might have big shoes to fill at that.

3. How much heat will John Tortorella bring?

If you thought the coach was ornery and demanding last season, you haven't seen anything yet. In a season in which expectations are the highest in franchise history, Tortorella will likely turn up the intensity. There is a fine line between encouragement and browbeating that the coach did well not to cross last season. Allies such as associate coach Craig Ramsay and players Tim Taylor and Dave Andreychuk will again act as buffers.

4. How much does Andreychuk have left at 40?

The question is prompted more by his September 29 birthday than concerns about his ability. Andreychuk, in his 22nd season, looks lean and mean after a summer workout program, and he said his enthusiasm is as high as ever. Good news for the still young Lightning.

Defensemen Janne Laukkanen skates during a scrimmage against fellow Lightning players at training camp at the Ice Sports Forum in Brandon. DIRK SHADD/ST. PETERSBURG TIMES

5. Is Dan Boyle a one-hit wonder?

Boyle brought it up unsolicited when he signed his new contract. He was fifth in the league among defensemen with 53 points and tied for second with nine power-play goals. He also was plus-9. In 170 previous games, Boyle had 59 points with five power-play goals and was minus-32. A two-year, $5.05-million deal makes the query even more pertinent.

6. Will Martin St. Louis and Eric Perrin rekindle their collegiate magic?

Playing on the same line for four years, they became the University of Vermont's top two all-time scorers. Perrin never had a legitimate shot at making an NHL team and played in Finland the past three seasons. The Lightning will give him his chance.

7. Who will be the fourth-line center?

Rookie Alexander Svitov played there last season, but he struggled and stayed with the Lightning, at least in part because Tampa Bay did not like the coaching situation at AHL Springfield. Svitov has big-time skills, but he is still raw and will get a stiff challenge from Martin Cibak, one of the organization's most defensively responsible players.

8. Can Janne Laukkanen's left hip take the strain?

If the arthritic joint is sound (and Laukkanen, 33, said it is after arthroscopic surgery), he has the skating ability and skill to man the point on the power play and give the team another puck carrier to help clear the defensive zone.

9. Is Eero Somervuori the hotshot he was made out to be?

A similar question follows rookie defenseman Andreas Holmqvist. But Somervuori is more intriguing because he is 24, was signed as part of the attempt to compensate for losing Prospal and last season became a legitimate star in his native Finland. Still, at 5-foot-10, 185 pounds, he is relatively small which makes any transition to the rougher North American game more problematic.

10. Is this team better than last season?

With basically the same lineup the Lightning will again will be a scrappy, in-your-face bunch. If Khabibulin returns to the form that made him one of the world's best in 2001-02, Tampa Bay will be difficult to beat.

THREE STRAIGHT GOALS, 6-0 MARK

TOM JONES

Not all hockey victories can be found in a textbook. Not every one follows a specific game plan or script. They aren't always delivered in nice tidy packages with cute little bows.

Despite the best and tireless efforts by coaches and the robotic, monotonous practices by the players, the way victories are drawn up on chalkboards and the way they turn out on the ice often are two entirely different things.

The good news for the Lightning is both count the same.

For the first time in six games this season, the Lightning shunned conventional victory and didn't jump out to a lead. But for the sixth time in six games, they were ahead when it counted: at the end. The Lightning set a franchise record for consecutive victories by climbing out of a two-goal, first-period hole and beating the Minnesota Wild 3-2 in front of 16,223 at the St. Pete Times Forum.

Before the game, Lightning coach John Tortorella talked about his team, still taking its baby steps down the path of victory, and the method of learning to win games that come in different shapes and sizes.

A few hours later, the Lightning added a little variety to their winning ways by falling behind 2-0 to a team it never had beaten in five tries. Instead of panicking, switching gears, abandoning their game plan, the Lightning simply hunkered down and fought their way back.

"I like the way they handled themselves," Tortorella said. "They didn't break apart. It's a good test for us to see how we handled the situation being down. We haven't been there that much this year."

	1st	2nd	3rd	T
Minnesota	2	0	0	**2**
Tampa Bay	0	2	1	**3**

Not much? Try 10 minutes, 10 seconds against New Jersey.

But when the Wild scored a pair of power-play goals less than a minute apart midway through the first period, the Lightning were down by two for the first time this season.

"We knew we had plenty of hockey left," Lightning forward Brad Richards said. "Forty minutes is a long time in hockey. We felt like we were playing well. We just had to get it going."

Richards got it going, scoring the key goal only 11 seconds into the second period.

"A huge goal," said Vinny Lecavalier, who then tied the score on the power play at 15:28 of the second period.

All that was left was the finishing touch, which was provided by Cory Stillman, who scored his team-leading fifth goal at 1:14 of the third period. With the Lightning short-handed, Stillman worked a two-on-one with Tim Taylor and scored the winner by snapping a wrist shot over the left shoulder of Wild goalie Manny Fernandez.

"I was thinking about going with a one-timer, but then I decided to take the shot I wanted to take," Stillman said. "That's the one I wanted."

That's the one the Lightning needed as they became just the 14th team to start a season with six consecutive victories. What made this one so tasty, though, was it didn't come easy.

"We had to work for this one after we put ourselves in a hole," said defenseman Dan Boyle, who had a pair of assists. "This is a tough team to play against when they get the lead, but we didn't panic. That's important. It's important to win games like this when not everything goes your way."

The Wild appear to be a shadow of the team that raced to the Western Conference final last season. But though they are missing key players, in particular leading scorer Marian Gaborik (contract dispute), they still play a stifling defensive style that is practically impossible to beat when a team falls behind.

October Results			
Fri. Oct. 10	Boston	W 5-1	1-0-0-0
Thu. Oct. 16	Phoenix	W 5-1	2-0-0-0
Sat. Oct. 18	at New Jersey	W 3-2	3-0-0-0
Tue. Oct. 21	Atlanta	W (OT) 3-2	4-0-0-0
Thu. Oct. 23	at Columbus	W 1-0	5-0-0-0
Sat. Oct. 25	Minnesota	W 3-2	6-0-0-0
Thu. Oct. 30	San Jose	T 2-2	6-0-1-0

The Lightning, though, found a way.

"They think they can win," Tortorella said. "Again, they're still in the process of learning how to win. That is another part of that process."

Ruslan Fedotenko (17) takes a shot but is taken down by Minnesota's Brad Bombardir. The Lightning beat the Wild, 3-2, and remain undefeated. DAN MCDUFFIE/ST. PETERSBURG TIMES

HEAD COACH JOHN TORTORELLA

The Lightning should hang a sign outside their locker room on days Coach John Tortorella calls for a video session: Check thin skin at the door.

Tampa Bay's sessions are a mixture of brutal honesty (the tapes don't lie) and critical evaluations by the coaches.

There can be heated exchanges as players and staff debate the debits and credits of plays. And there can be hurt feelings when players take as insults Tortorella's "correcting."

But the sessions also are for encouragement. A player shown making a bonehead play one minute can be shown making a marvelous one the next.

"I don't want you to think it's all just pounding them, but I show what happens," Tortorella said. "The beauty of tape is it's right there and then you get into a discussion. The bottom line is to resolve problems going on on the ice or with players."

If feelings are hurt along the way, so be it.

"This is a man's game," Tortorella said. "If your ego gets bruised just by simple correcting, then you're in the wrong sport."

Tortorella has been a video wonk since taking over the Lightning in January 2001. Sessions occur the day before games and are 20 to 45 minutes.

Those first sessions were difficult. Players not used to seeing mistakes exposed in front of teammates resented the spotlight. But Tortorella said he does not choose clips based on the players involved but on the mistakes he is trying to address. It's the same for good plays.

Named Coach: January 6, 2001
Born: June 24, 1958

"If it's good we're going to show you, but if it's a mistake you're pretty much on the carpet," Tortorella said. "Players don't like that in a group setting. But group settings are great because everybody sees the mistakes and they'll try to stay away from them."

And though some players still have trouble with the group thing, most have bought in.

"Before you were just hoping you didn't show up on the video, so you just kind of sat there and were quiet and hoped everything passed," defenseman Cory Sarich said. "The only way to get better is knowing what you did wrong and coming to grips with we all make mistakes. Becoming accountable is what has happened in our video sessions."

Some of that is because the players better understand Tortorella's system. But Tortorella and the players also have a better relationship.

"It's a mutual respect," center Tim Taylor said. "That doesn't develop over one year, but you gain that respect for each other and you know what the other is thinking. So when the coach yells at you, you know he's not coming down on you. He wants to win for the team and for everyone."

Tortorella handles five-on-five play. He breaks down only Lightning video.

"I'm not five positive, five negative," Tortorella said. "I don't even consider it negative. It's correcting. The tape talks to me. I show what we see."

No one is spared. Even captain Dave Andreychuk showed up on the negative side as the team prepared for the game against the Coyotes at the St. Pete Times Forum.

Andreychuk, though, fires back if he does not agree with Tortorella's critique.

"He has the final decision, but you can tell him what you're thinking, and that's when it might get a little heated," Andreychuk said.

Tortorella loves that.

"If you have a beef, argue with me," he said.

Andreychuk said he sometimes asks questions just to get a discussion going.

"So he can explain things a bit better," Andreychuk said. "I might ask why he thinks that, but only to make sure the point is made to everybody."

Thick skin takes longer to penetrate. —DAMIAN CRISTODERO

Head coach John Tortorella argues a call behind the Lightning bench. DIRK SHADD/ST. PETERSBURG TIMES

A ROUT LIKE NO OTHER

TOM JONES

The Lightning have played 900 games that have counted in the National Hockey League: 883 regular-season games and 17 playoff games.

Browse the record books, or ask any diehard fan, and learn that the majority fall somewhere between "heartbreaking" and "downright embarrassing." Among the 900, there has been a modest share of good games.

But the best game in franchise history? The absolute best out of all the games dating to the first on October 7, 1992?

The argument can be made: The Lightning played their best game ever. This can't be argued: The Lightning never scored as many goals or beat a team as badly as they did when they defeated the Penguins 9-0.

"This was our night," Lightning center Vinny Lecavalier said. "Everything went our way."

The funny thing is, the game looked like it had all the makings of a dense speed bump, a kind of game that could spoil the Lightning's good vibe.

The Penguins, missing their best player (Mario Lemieux) and sitting their hotshot young goalie (Marc-Andre Fleury), have perhaps the worst team in the league. Toss in this: Tampa Bay, off to its best start, was ripe to be a little too big for its britches and a little too musty after playing for the ninth time at home in 11 games.

Lightning coach John Tortorella summed up the matchup with one word: "dangerous."

But instead of peeking through the cracks of his fingers, Tortorella watched a game in which the Lightning bullied an opponent like never before.

When exactly did the Lightning know that something special was brewing?

"I think right from go," Lecavalier said. "We came out to play."

	1st	2nd	3rd	T
Pittsburgh	0	0	0	**0**
Tampa Bay	2	3	4	**9**

The Lightning never stopped. Lecavalier netted his third career hat trick, goalie Nikolai Khabibulin tied the franchise record for shutouts and the Lightning showed no mercy in a performance so dominating that it was hard for the 18,262 at the St. Pete Times Forum to not feel sorry for the Lemieux-less Penguins.

"By no means are you trying to run it up against any team in the National Hockey League," Tortorella said. "I have a lot of respect for the Penguins and that coaching staff. But you can't tell your players to stop playing. We just caught them on the right night."

Though the Lightning can't come out and say it, this game proved they can be good enough to knock the fillings out of an opponent.

"Well, I don't know what it does for the confidence of the team," said center Cory Stillman, who had a goal and three assists, "but it helps the confidence of the guys who were involved in the scoring."

He could've been talking about Ruslan Fedotenko, who had his first two goals of the season to close the scoring. He could've been talking about Alexander Svitov, who picked up his first point of the season. Heck, he could've been talking about just about everyone. Of the Lightning's 18 skaters, 13 picked up a point.

"It feels good to do something like this, but really, I don't care if we win 2-1 or 9-0," Lecavalier said. "You're trying to go out there and embarrass anybody, but it's got to help the confidence of a lot of people."

Tortorella still was a tad nervous midway through the game. The Lightning got a big boost by killing off a seven-minute Penguins power play in the first period, but led only 2-0 halfway through the second. Lecavalier then turned the game for good when he scored on a short-handed breakaway, the first of his three goals, to start the rout.

It was 5-0 at the end of two and then 8-0 before Penguins rookie coach Ed Olczyk mercifully pulled backup goalie Sebastien Caron when Fedotenko scored 8:40 into the third.

Meantime, Khabibulin picked up his 12th shutout in a Lightning uniform to tie Daren Puppa's franchise record, though he barely had to work as the Lightning outshot Pittsburgh 42-15.

"This is about as bad as it can get," Olczyk said.

For the Lightning, it's as good as it ever has been, but as early as the second period, Tortorella was hoping his team can re-focus for the game at Carolina.

November Results			
Sat. Nov. 1	Carolina	W 4-3	7-0-1-0
Tue. Nov. 4	Washington	L 5-1	7-1-1-0
Thu. Nov. 6	Los Angeles	L (OT) 1-0	7-1-1-1
Sat. Nov. 8	Pittsburgh	W 9-0	8-1-1-1
Sun. Nov. 9	at Carolina	T 1-1	8-1-2-1
Tue. Nov. 11	at Florida	L 4-0	8-2-2-1
Fri. Nov. 14	at Washington	W 5-2	9-2-2-1
Thu. Nov. 20	NY Islanders	W 3-2	10-2-2-1
Sat. Nov. 22	Buffalo	W 2-1	11-2-2-1
Sun. Nov. 23	at Carolina	T 0-0	11-2-3-1
Tue. Nov. 25	NY Rangers	L 2-0	11-3-3-1
Fri. Nov. 28	St. Louis	T 2-2	11-3-4-1
Sat. Nov. 29	at Atlanta	L 2-1	11-4-4-1

"We can't take any of these goals with us," Tortorella said. "[Today] we start 0-0. But I trust my team to stay focused. They know [today] is another game."

But it's on the heels of what might have been the best Lightning game ever.

Lightning center Vincent Lecavalier celebrates after scoring to complete a hat trick against Pittsburgh in the third period. The Penguins were shut out 9-0. STEPHEN J. CODDINGTON/ST. PETERSBURG TIMES

DROUGHTS AND SKIDS CEASE FOR LIGHTNING

DAMIAN CRISTODERO

It was just one game. Lightning coach John Tortorella will hammer that into his players' heads.

It wasn't even a very artistic game, what with its grinding demeanor, the fighting and Tampa Bay's need for a comeback after blowing a two-goal lead late in the second period.

But considering the freefall in which the team recently found itself, The 5-4 overtime victory over the Flyers at the Wachovia Center was a thing of beauty.

"It was a big character win," right wing Martin St. Louis said.

Said captain Dave Andreychuk: "I believe this is a game we will look back on and know we can win in a tough building."

The toughest. Even with the loss, Philadelphia is the league's best home team with 27 points and a 12-2-2-1 record. And the Flyers, with 44 points, entered as the No. 1 team in the league.

Who would have guessed it was the perfect setup for the Lightning to break a four-game losing streak and for their biggest scorers to finally, finally, break out?

St. Louis scored twice. He tied it at four with 8:02 left in the third and won it 2:03 into overtime.

Vinny Lecavalier, Brad Richards and Cory Stillman also scored to break long droughts.

Goalie Nikolai Khabibulin needs to work on his puck handling as he gave away two goals with misplays. But he was otherwise strong with 37 saves for his second victory in 12 decisions against the Flyers (2-10-0).

	1st	2nd	3rd	OT	T
Tampa Bay	1	1	2	1	5
Philadelphia	0	1	3	0	4

And how about Andre Roy and Chris Dingman, who fought Donald Brashear and Jim Vandermeer, respectively, in the game's first 16 seconds to set an undeniable tone?

"That's the team I thought we saw earlier in the year and quite a bit of last year," Tortorella said. "We made mistakes and it was ugly by both teams. But that's the way we won last year."

A few more notables before getting to the nitty-gritty.

The Lightning are 3-8-2 in their past 13. But they had just 18 goals in their past 12 and the five against the Flyers were the most since Tampa Bay got five November 14 against the Capitals. The Lightning also had two power-play goals in a game for the first time since October 30 against the Sharks to slow an 8-for-93 skid.

Lecavalier's power-play goal was his 11th but first in eight games. Richards' goal was his fourth and first in 14 games as was Stillman's 11th.

"Our support guys were there, too, but what kicks in tonight is some of our better players did some good things at important times," Tortorella said.

One of Tampa Bay's best players did a couple of bad things during a 9:01 stretch that began with 52.8 seconds left in the second and ended 8:08 into the third with four Flyers goals.

Tony Amonte scored 21 seconds after Richards to make it 2-1. Mark Recchi scored 19 seconds into the third into an open net to tie at two thanks to Khabibulin's terrible giveaway behind the goal line.

Stillman made it 3-2 at 5:08, but Michal Handzus tied it 15 seconds later on his own rebound of a wrap-around attempt. Jeremy Roenick made it 4-3 at 8:08 after Khabibulin's backhand pass behind the net hand-cuffed defenseman Cory Sarich and bounced to Roenick for an easy goal.

"It's an amazing thing," Flyers coach Ken Hitchcock said. "The game never really changes. It's all about what you give up."

Or for the Lightning, what you take in overtime. Stillman outfought two Flyers for the puck along the center-ice boards and sent a chip pass to Andreychuk, who passed cross-ice to St. Louis.

The right wing scored his eighth but only his second in 15 games.

"We were up, we were down, we won it in overtime," St. Louis said. "It's nice to push and get some results."

December Results			
Tue. Dec. 2	at Montreal	L 3-2	11-5-4-1
Thu. Dec. 4	Ottawa	L 4-1	11-6-4-1
Sat. Dec. 6	at Buffalo	W 3-1	12-6-4-1
Sun. Dec. 7	at NY Rangers	W 3-2	13-6-4-1
Tue. Dec. 9	at NY Islanders	L 5-2	13-7-4-1
Thu. Dec. 11	at Ottawa	L 3-2	13-8-4-1
Sat. Dec. 13	Montreal	L 5-2	13-9-4-1
Tue. Dec. 16	at Toronto	L 3-0	13-10-4-1
Thu. Dec. 18	at Philadelphia	W (OT) 5-4	14-10-4-1
Sat. Dec. 20	Dallas	L 2-1	14-11-4-1
Tue. Dec. 23	at Boston	T 1-1	14-11-5-1
Fri. Dec. 26	at Atlanta	L 3-1	14-12-5-1
Sat. Dec. 27	Boston	W 4-2	15-12-5-1
Mon. Dec. 29	Anaheim	L 2-0	15-13-5-1
Wed. Dec. 31	Florida	T 2-2	15-13-6-1

"To start a streak or start feeling good about yourself, you have to win, so this is one. Hopefully we can build on it," Tortorella said. "But it is just one game."

Told you so.

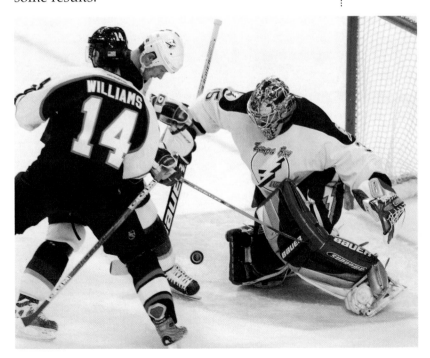

Nikolai Khabibulin blocks a shot as Philadelphia's Justin Williams and Tampa Bay's Nolan Pratt battle for the rebound in front of the net. The Lightning won in overtime, 5-4. AP/WWP

#22 DAN BOYLE

A s a bit of an intense perfectionist himself, Lightning coach John Tortorella could tell that Dan Boyle was getting frustrated. The 27-year-old defenseman takes a lot of responsibility upon himself, a trait Tortorella likes, but when Boyle's scoring touch vanished in the first 18 games of the season, the strain began to show.

"He wants to score goals," Tortorella said. "He thinks that's a big part of his game for this team to win and it is."

With two goals in the Lightning's last two games and enough fisticuff action to vent any amount of frustration, Boyle has reclaimed his niche and provided the struggling offense a lift.

"It was bothering me," Boyle said of the 32-game goal-less streak that began at the end of the last regular season. "I put a lot of pressure on myself and I'll always be like that. That's just the type person I am."

It's the type Tortorella has come to respect since Boyle was obtained from the Florida Panthers for a fifth-round draft pick in January 2002.

Boyle set career highs last season in goals (13), assists (40), points (53), games (77) and plus-minus (plus-9) and led the Lightning with an average ice time of 24:30. He began this season doing many of the same things, except scoring goals. Boyle has two goals and nine assists this season and leads the team with 23:26 in average ice time.

"Danny is a guy I have a tremendous amount of respect for in the way he has improved in his mental toughness and his battling since the first time we picked him up," Tortorella said. "When we first got him, he thought he was playing [pickup] hockey and wasn't involved at all. He's probably one of our most involved guys right now, and I think getting a little bit of result will help him.

"We want Danny Boyle to be instinctive because that's what his strength is. Maybe if a puck or two goes in the net, it will allow him to just go and that's when Danny is at his best."

Boyle said he was creating enough opportunities to be happy with his last seven games but needed to shoot more. He averaged just 1.6 shots through the first 18 games and scored on his only shot of the game in a 2-2 tie against St. Louis. He had four shots and the only Lightning score in a 2-1 loss at Atlanta.

Height: 5'11"
Weight: 190
Position: D
Shoots: Right
Born: July 12, 1976
Ottawa, Ontario

Tortorella theorizes the two goals will allow Boyle to relax.

"I think he is a great team guy," Tortorella said. "I think when he feels he is not producing for the team, he adds even more pressure on himself and starts overthinking."

Boyle is hardly a ruffian, but a first-period run-in with St. Louis' Mike Danton sparked a night of aggression. Boyle drew two five-minute fighting majors and in the overtime was tussling with Blues center Doug Weight.

"You have to let guys know that you have their back," Boyle said. "That's kind of one of the ways to show it. You have to let a teammate know if someone messes with you, I'll be right there for you. It's like a trust thing."

And a signal to the bench that not only select players need to sacrifice some blood to change the game.

"I don't think it always needs to be Andre [Roy]," Tortorella said. "I don't think it should always be [Chris Dingman] and players like that. Even some of your offensive players, when they're struggling like they are right now, they need to get involved in some of that stuff. It's amazing what it does to the bench when they see some of what I guess you would consider your best players statistics-wise get involved that way. It provides a big lift and it helps a team."

Boyle has that part covered. —BRANT JAMES

AVALANCHE TRIP; LIGHTNING FALL

DAMIAN CRISTODERO

You could not have asked for better window dressing for a hockey game.

The Lightning faced the Avalanche in front of a pulsating crowd of 19,212 at the St. Pete Times Forum that made the game feel as if it should have been played in the postseason.

A national television audience watched on ESPN2, and the teams stayed in overdrive throughout, trading slap shots and body shots. And for only the third time in NHL history a regular-season game ended on an overtime penalty shot.

Too bad for the Lightning they came out on the short end of a 5-4 decision. The final blow being Milan Hejduk's second goal of the game 59 seconds into extra time.

Still... "That was an exciting hockey game," Lightning coach John Tortorella said. "We enjoyed watching it on the bench. The building was great, national TV. It was an exciting hockey game."

Tampa Bay's point for the regulation tie gave it 50 and a four-point advantage in the Southeast with two games in hand on the second-place Thrashers.

Then again... Tampa Bay could not hold the 4-3 third-period lead it built with a three-goal second. Players said they may have laid back some in the third period. And Hejduk's first goal, which tied the score with 6:19 left, beat Nikolai Khabibulin on the short side.

"We need a save in the third period," Tortorella said. "Plain and simple."

And talk about a buzz kill. Hejduk's winner smothered a crowd that shook the building

	1st	2nd	3rd	OT	T
Colorado	2	1	1	1	5
Tampa Bay	1	3	0	0	4

imploring goalie Khabibulin to make a game-saving stop.

"It was an interesting finish," said Hejduk, who had a game-high four points and was awarded the penalty shot after Lightning defenseman Brad Lukowich, without a choice, hauled him down from behind on a breakaway. "It was kind of a roller-coaster game."

"An exciting game," Avalanche coach Tony Granato said. "That team threw everything at us that they could."

He wasn't kidding.

Tampa Bay outshot Colorado 35-24, including 17-6 in the first period. And Colorado goalie David Aebischer was solid with 31 saves, including a huge stop on Dan Boyle in overtime.

Tampa Bay did its damage in the second, turning a 2-1 deficit into a 4-3 lead with goals by Dmitry Afanasenkov, Tim Taylor and Ruslan Fedotenko. Fedotenko's goal, with 2:54 left, put the Lightning up by one.

But Martin St. Louis said he felt the tide turn as the third period progressed.

"I'll take a point any night against that Colorado team," the right wing said. "But in terms of the way we were playing in the third period, it's like we were sitting back. We were waiting for them to put it in the back of the net."

As for Hejduk's goal, Khabibulin said he did not cheat off the post.

"It's one of those games I have to give credit to the shooters," Khabibulin said. "They picked the corners tonight."

Hejduk said that was the plan.

"We knew he was a butterfly goalie and he goes down," he said. "We tried to shoot high as soon as possible."

Joe Sakic's short-handed goal that tied the score at one was the only Avalanche goal that did not graze the crossbar as Martin Skuola, Alex Tanguay and Hejduk all sent lasers into the corners of the net.

"Every goal they got were on good shots," Khabibulin said.

Just what you would expect from a team that entered tied for the No. 2 spot in the league. The Lightning's disappointment was made more acute by the two third-period goals they allowed in their 2-1 loss to the Panthers.

"We can't have letdowns any time in the third up by a goal," St. Louis said.

"But we played a good hockey game," Tortorella said. "We just couldn't hold them off at the end."

January Results			
Fri. Jan. 2	Columbus	L 2-0	15-14-6-1
Sat. Jan. 3	Philadelphia	W 6-1	16-14-6-1
Tue. Jan. 6	at Ottawa	L 5-2	16-15-6-1
Thu. Jan. 8	at Montreal	W 4-1	17-15-6-1
Fri. Jan. 9	at New Jersey	W 4-1	18-15-6-1
Sun. Jan. 11	at NY Rangers	W (OT) 2-1	19-15-6-1
Tue. Jan. 13	at Pittsburgh	W 3-1	20-15-6-1
Thu. Jan. 15	Carolina	W 5-4	21-15-6-1
Sat. Jan. 17	at Florida	L 2-1	21-16-6-1
Mon. Jan. 19	Colorado	L (OT) 5-4	21-16-6-2
Wed. Jan. 21	at Vancouver	L (OT) 5-4	21-16-6-3
Thu. Jan. 22	at Edmonton	W 3-2	22-16-6-3
Sat. Jan. 24	at Calgary	W 6-2	23-16-6-3
Tue. Jan. 27	at Pittsburgh	W 6-2	24-16-6-3
Thu. Jan. 29	Pittsburgh	W 5-1	25-16-6-3
Sat. Jan. 31	Atlanta	W 5-2	26-16-6-3

Goalie Nikolai Khabibulin tries to make a save on Colorado's Milan Hejduk. Hejduk received a tripping call on the play and won the game with the penalty shot.
DIRK SHADD/ST. PETERSBURG TIMES

CHECK ANOTHER GOAL OFF THE LIST

TOM JONES

	1st	2nd	3rd	T
Florida	1	0	1	**2**
Tampa Bay	1	2	0	**3**

Tampa Bay is practically a lock to win the Southeast Division and make its second straight showing in the Stanley Cup playoffs. That's all the team really cares about and all that really matters.

But even though Tampa Bay is in the midst of one of the hottest stretches in team history, there was one item left to cross off on the team's checklist to make this regular season complete.

Beat those Florida Panthers, a team that badgers the Lightning and their fans as no other regardless of the standings.

Check it off: The Lightning finally ended Florida and goaltender Robert Luongo's hex against it with a 3-2 victory before an announced 18,888 at the St. Pete Times Forum.

Yeah, sure, ho-hum, the players tried to slough off the victory.

"Just another two points," right wing Martin St. Louis said.

"We don't care who we play," center Vinny Lecavalier said. "Every night we want to win."

But let's be honest, the Lightning wanted this one. Bad.

Forget for a moment that the Lightning increased their lead in the Southeast to 16 points over the Panthers, pretty much burying Florida's hopes in the division. Or that it improved to 9-1-1 in the past 11 games and 14-2-1-2 since January 8.

This game carried a little extra juice for the Lightning because it is, after all, Lightning-Panthers, a rivalry with 11 years of nasty baggage before the added spice of this season. Now behind the Panthers bench is former Lightning assistant John Torchetti and former Lightning coach Steve Ludzik, while former Lightning GM Rick Dudley is the boss in Florida.

Then consider the Lightning was winless (0-2-1) this season against its cross-state rival.

"It's a team that—I don't want to call it a rivalry. I still think you need to play some games in the playoffs before you call it a rivalry—but it's a team that we haven't been able to beat for one reason or another," Lightning coach John Tortorella said.

The reason? Luongo, who stopped 90 of 93 shots in the past two meetings, including a remarkable 50-save performance in a 2-1 Florida victory last month.

"He has given us trouble in the past," St. Louis said.

Trouble? More like fits.

But the Lightning ended Luongo's mastery with goals by Lecavalier, St. Louis and Cory Sarich.

Lecavalier's goal at 13:06 of the first opened the scoring and gave the sixth-year professional 20 goals for the fifth consecutive season.

"I'm not satisfied with 20, obviously," Lecavalier said. "But at this point of the season with the month of December I had [three goals in 15 games], it's nice."

Meantime, St. Louis' league-leading seventh short-handed goal—his 14th short-handed goal with the Lightning to tie the franchise record set by Rob Zamuner—was a dagger. It extended Tampa Bay's lead to 3-1 late in the second period and took some steam out of Tortorella's postgame anger.

Tortorella was riled because St. Louis' goal came while Tampa Bay was serving its second too-many-men-on-the-ice penalty of the period. It wasn't a fluke. The Lightning have been nabbed 15 times for having too many men, second in the NHL to Calgary's 16.

"It's just beyond belief how many too-many-men-on-the-ice penalties we take," Tortorella said. "We have to be going for the world record. It's just ridiculous, and it has to stop. Those are the ones you don't kill off, especially two in one game, and we end up scoring a short-handed goal. That's a huge goal. It should be in our net."

But other than that and a late Florida charge that cut the lead to 3-2 and made for a tense final five minutes, the Lightning stayed hot and held on behind goalie John Grahame's 29 saves.

"We found a way to get it done," said Tortorella, who had high praise for the Panthers and Torchetti.

Considering the opponent, getting it done was more than good enough for the Lightning.

February Results			
Mon. Feb. 2	at Philadelphia	W 2-1	27-16-6-3
Tue. Feb. 3	at Washington	L 2-1	27-17-6-3
Thu. Feb. 5	at Nashville	W 5-2	28-17-6-3
Tue. Feb. 10	Toronto	T 4-4	28-17-7-3
Thu. Feb. 12	Montreal	W 5-3	29-17-7-3
Sat. Feb. 14	Florida	W 3-2	30-17-7-3
Tue. Feb. 17	Philadelphia	W 5-2	31-17-7-3
Thu. Feb. 19	at St. Louis	L (OT) 4-3	31-17-7-4
Fri. Feb. 20	at Buffalo	L (OT) 4-3	31-17-7-5
Mon. Feb. 23	at Washington	W 6-3	32-17-7-5
Wed. Feb. 25	at Atlanta	W 4-2	33-17-7-5
Thu. Feb. 26	Toronto	W 4-3	34-17-7-5
Sat. Feb. 28	Washington	W 4-2	35-17-7-5

John Grahame makes a save during second-period action against the Florida Panthers. The Lightning held on to their second-period lead to win the game, 3-2. DIRK SHADD/ST. PETERSBURG TIMES

#4 VINCENT LECAVALIER

Vinny Lecavalier believes the Lightning can finish second in the East. Heck, even first place isn't out of the question.

It's a simple equation. Tampa Bay is comfortably ahead in the Southeast with 70 points, six behind No. 2 Toronto and 10 behind the Flyers with one and two games in hand, respectively.

Win those games, Lecavalier said, and anything can happen.

"It's a goal for sure," he said. "At the beginning of the year, it was to make the playoffs and to finish first in our division. Now it's to catch up for second or even first. The way we're playing right now, you never know."

Pretty big talk from Lecavalier. But that's what happens when one's confidence soars.

The native of Ile-Bizard, Quebec, has five goals and five assists in a six-game points streak. He has seven goals and 10 assists and is plus-13 in his past 11 games and was named the league's Offensive Player of the Week for the week ending February 15.

Lecavalier had four goals and three assists in three games as the Lightning went 2-0-1.

Since Lecavalier got hot, the team is 9-1-1.

"He's more intense," right wing Martin St. Louis said. "He wants it more right now. And when Vinny is intense, he's one of the best players in the league."

It is as if the previous 34 games, in which Lecavalier had five goals, eight assists and was minus-6, never happened.

What has happened is Lecavalier, 23, has found a comfort zone on a line with St. Louis and left wing Ruslan Fedotenko. And he and the coach, with whom he has a sometimes contentious relationship, are in a better place.

Coach John Tortorella has gotten more involved studying video with Lecavalier, and Lecavalier has been watching and listening. After their session before the January 21 game against the Canucks, Lecavalier predicted he would have "a great second half" of the season.

Coach and player had at least one other personalized session, and more likely will take place.

Height:	6'4"
Weight:	207
Position:	C
Shoots:	Left
Born:	April 20, 1980
	Ile-Bizard, Quebec

"Any time you work together, you're going to get more results," Lecavalier said. "Obviously, you get a better relationship out of that. We're in a good situation right now. We're winning and having fun. When you work together, it's just going to get better."

"I understand him better, and I think he understands me better," Tortorella said. "It's a much better line of communication."

As for the on-ice product, Tortorella said, "We feel he knows what we want with our team concept. It's a matter of being prepared mentally to do it more consistently. That's what is happening, and his production is rising because of it."

Whereas Lecavalier used to regularly glide over the blue line and give up the puck with a too-cute pass, he now churns his legs and tries to beat defenders with his speed.

He shoots more (26 in his past five games), is back checking more consistently and against the Canadiens carried the puck off the side wall into the slot and fed St. Louis at the side of the net for Tampa Bay's first goal.

"That is two years in the making, trying to make him attack that seam," Tortorella said. "He attacked that seam, and things opened up all over the place. It comes down to mental maturity."

"I haven't done that in a while," said Lecavalier, who has 20 goals, 21 assists and is plus-11. "It worked. Any time you go through the box, a lot of things happen."

They need to keep happening if the team wants to move up in the standings starting with the game against the Flyers at the St. Pete Times Forum.

"There are still 25 games left," Lecavalier said. "We have to make sure we finish the season strong." —DAMIAN CRISTODERO

The home crowd goes wild behind fan favorite Vincent Lecavalier. DIRK SHADD/ST. PETERSBURG TIMES

LIGHTNING NEAR TOP SEED IN EAST

FRANK PASTOR

To Vinny Lecavalier, a goal is a goal, whether it's the puck that went in off an opponent's skate in the victory over New Jersey or the two highlight-reel goals he tallied in the 4-1 win over Washington.

"It doesn't matter how you do it," Lecavalier said. "When you score on a breakaway, it doesn't count as two. It counts as one. Same thing with a rebound, a garbage goal. It's just as good."

Especially when the stakes are so high.

With its franchise-record 23rd home win of the season before an announced 18,812 at the St. Pete Times Forum, Tampa Bay ran its point total to 103, four more than Boston and five more than Philadelphia in the Eastern Conference. With three games left, the Flyers can pick up only six more points. The Bruins, with four contests remaining, can add as many as eight.

The race for the Presidents' Trophy is even tighter. With a 2-0 victory over Colorado, Detroit remains tied with Tampa Bay for the overall lead in points and wins (44), though the Red Wings have a game in hand.

The Lightning outworked the Capitals from beginning to end, outshooting them 32-22 and avoiding any apparent lapses as they readied their game for the playoffs.

"We just want to stay away from bad habits and just continue to work on our game," Coach John Tortorella said.

Lecavalier scored twice on odd-man rushes, and Brad Richards had two points to tie his season high of 75. Richards set a franchise record with his 190th assist, one more than Brian Bradley.

	1st	2nd	3rd	T
Washington	0	0	1	1
Tampa Bay	1	2	1	4

Tim Taylor picked up his career-high 15th assist, and Nikolai Khabibulin had a shutout for more than two periods before finishing with 21 saves.

The Lightning are playing at such a high level, newcomer Eric Perrin noticed the difference immediately in his first game since being recalled from Hershey of the American Hockey League.

"It's incredible how they come out of their zone with such control and patience, and they just do the little things right," Perrin said. "It's just chip the puck, get it deep when you've got nothing, make the simple play. And I think that's what makes this team really good.

"Once they get down there, they're such a fast team, and they've got a great forecheck. And then once they get that puck down low, teams can't control them. It's great to watch."

No one was more fun to watch than Lecavalier, who moved within one goal of his career high of 33 set last season. Though he has been frustrated on breakaway opportunities in the past, Lecavalier buried his chance against the Capitals.

"Vinny's confident. Vinny's fine," Tortorella said. "He has that offensive instinct where he does end up with a lot of breakaways. He scored some important goals tonight."

Lecavalier opened the scoring 9:15 into the first period. Skating down the right wing on a two-on-one with Fredrik Modin, Lecavalier faked a pass, freezing defenseman Josef Boumedienne, switched to his backhand as he moved around goalie Matthew Yeats and shoveled a forehand shot into the net.

Lecavalier returned to the forehand-backhand-forehand move to give the Lightning a 2-0 lead 2:25 into the second. A puck that deflected off a defenseman's skate sprung Lecavalier, who skated uncontested into the slot.

With two pucks already behind Yeats, the Lightning stormed the rookie goaltender the rest of the period, outshooting the Capitals 13-4. Their work was rewarded when Modin redirected a Cory Stillman pass past Yeats with 2:17 left.

The play started with Richards' cross-ice pass to Stillman in the left circle. Stillman passed to Modin, who deflected the puck under the crossbar. Richards scored the Lightning's final goal when he followed his backhand shot 10:02 into the third.

"They're a great team offensively," said Yeats, who stopped 28 shots in his third NHL appearance. "They've got a lot of speed and just capital-

March/April Results			
Mon. March 1	at Colorado	W 3-0	36-17-7-5
Wed. March 3	at Chicago	W 5-3	37-17-7-5
Fri. March 5	New Jersey	W (OT) 3-2	38-17-7-5
Sat. March 6	at Florida	W 5-3	39-17-7-5
Mon. March 8	at Detroit	T 1-1	39-17-8-5
Wed. March 10	at Carolina	W 4-2	40-17-8-5
Fri. March 12	NY Rangers	W 5-2	41-17-8-5
Sat. March 13	Carolina	L 5-1	41-18-8-5
Tue. March 16	NY Islanders	L 3-1	41-19-8-5
Thu. March 18	Buffalo	W 3-1	42-19-8-5
Sat. March 20	at Boston	L 5-4	42-20-8-5
Sun. March 21	at NY Islanders	L 3-0	42-21-8-5
Tue. March 23	at Toronto	W 7-2	43-21-8-5
Thu. March 25	New Jersey	W 2-1	44-21-8-5
Sat. March 27	Washington	W 4-1	45-21-8-5
Mon. March 29	Ottawa	L (OT) 5-4	45-21-8-6
Thu. April 1	Florida	W 4-3	46-21-8-6
Sat. April 3	Atlanta	L 2-1	46-22-8-6

ize on turnovers. Most of their chances were Grade A chances, and it made a nice challenge for me."

The score could have been more lopsided, but Yeats stopped Dmitry Afanasenkov on a breakaway after Afanasenkov put the puck between defenseman Jean-Luc Grand-Pierre's legs. And Richards tipped a Martin St. Louis centering pass over the net, two of 10 scoring chances for the Lightning in the first.

Vincent Lecavalier (left) congratulates teammate Fredrik Modin after he scored the Lightning's third goal. Tampa Bay held the Capitals to one goal and won, 4-1. DAN MCDUFFIE/ST. PETERSBURG TIMES

LIGHTNING SEAL DEAL

DAMIAN CRISTODERO

You didn't have to ask Lightning president Ron Campbell how he felt. The huge smile on his face gave it away.

You didn't have to ask defenseman Brad Lukowich twice what he was thinking. The first question brought it all tumbling out.

That's what happens when you are No. 1, and that is where Tampa Bay finds itself.

The Lightning's 4-3 victory over the Panthers at the St. Pete Times Forum coupled with the Bruins' 3-3 tie with the Capitals clinched the top seed in the East and home ice through the first three rounds of the playoffs.

"It's something that no one ever thought we could do," Lukowich said. "To say, 'Yeah, we did it,' and to make all those doubters believe in us feels great."

"It's spectacular," Campbell said. "Who would have thunk it?"

How appropriate, then, that Martin St. Louis should have the leading role. The right wing, who almost four years ago was as unlikely a star as Tampa Bay was an elite team, scored twice in the third period, once short-handed, and got the winner, his team-record seventh, with 2:20 remaining.

It was St. Louis' first goals in seven games and gave him, with one game remaining, a team-high 37 and a league-high 93 points. That's seven ahead of Colorado's Joe Sakic, who has three games left.

No wonder Lukowich was chanting, literally, that St. Louis, with league highs of eight short-handed goals and 11 short-handed points, should be league MVP.

"He's the man," Lukowich said. "He was awesome."

There were other notables. Cory Stillman had three assists, including a nice play that kept the puck in the offensive zone and led to St. Louis' winning goal.

Brad Richards scored his 26th goal and had an assist. Fredrik Modin scored his 29th and goalie John Grahame made 29 saves despite having his left leg wrapped around the post in the second period in a collision with Florida defenseman Jay Bouwmeester. Grahame stayed down briefly but stayed in the game.

One downer. The Red Wings' 3-2 victory over the Blues clinched the President's Trophy with 109

Martin St. Louis flies past Panther goalie Steve Shields to score his team's third goal. DAN MCDUFFIE/ST. PETERSBURG TIMES

points, one more than Tampa Bay can get if it wins against Atlanta.

The Bruins, with two games remaining, could still match the Lightning's 106 points, but Tampa Bay holds all the tiebreakers. Tampa Bay's first-round opponent could be the Islanders, Canadiens or Sabres.

"Good for them," Coach John Tortorella said of his players. "You win your division and now you win your conference [in the regular season]. Two or three years ago who would have thought that. And the credit goes to the guys in the locker room. They stayed together and accomplished a couple of nice things here. Now that's done with. Now it's on to bigger and better things."

"Bottom line, we didn't play a 60-minute game," Panthers coach John Torchetti said. "They played 60 minutes."

They played 20, anyway. Florida led 2-1 after two periods and had a 25-15 shot advantage. Notable because the Panthers had allowed an average 34.6 shots and a league-high 2,796.

"We know we're not as juiced as we are against a team like Ottawa," Tortorella said. "It's a tough thing when you go through a grind, and you're not as on edge when you get involved in a grind like this. But still I don't think we weren't working hard enough."

Until the third period in which the Lightning scored three times. Modin tied the score at two, and St. Louis' short-handed goal made it 3-2. St. Louis stripped the puck from defenseman Lyle Odelein. Nice revenge after Odelein mashed St. Louis' face into the ice in the second period in front of referee Rob Martell, who did not make a call.

Odelein made it 3-3 with 5:46 left on a shot that bounced off Lukowich before it bounced past Grahame. But all that did was set up St. Louis' winner.

"It's big," St. Louis said of the No. 1 seed. "But if you don't do anything with it, it means nothing."

On this night, it meant everything.

Martin St. Louis celebrates after scoring the game-winning goal in the third period to clinch a playoff berth. DAN MCDUFFIE/ST. PETERSBURG TIMES

ROUND 1

Lightning Defeat NY Islanders, 4-1

Darryl Sydor rushes toward Martin St. Louis to celebrate St. Louis' game-winning overtime goal against the New York Islanders. The win in Game 5 sends them to the next round. DIRK SHADD/ST. PETERSBURG TIMES

#26 MARTIN ST. LOUIS

A wry smile and a knowing look is pretty much all Martin St. Louis would offer. Even after a game's worth of being clutched, poked, hacked and having his head plunged against the ice as if Lyle Odelein was unclogging a toilet, the Lightning right wing was not going to indulge in any postgame gloating. Even after scoring two goals, including the game winner. Even after he stole the puck from his tormentor and swooped in for his league-leading eighth short-handed goal of the season in an eventual 4-3 win against Florida.

Not so much as a ha!

St. Louis is not the type to express that kind of satisfaction. And he might as well save the one ha! he might have in his 5-foot-9 body for later. For as surely as the Lightning begin the Eastern Conference playoffs against the Islanders at the St. Pete Times Forum, St. Louis will be hounded and targeted not only as the league's leading scorer, but as an undersized player teams try to consume with physicality.

"It's going to get worse for him as far as the clutching and grabbing, but we don't worry about that with Marty," Lightning coach John Tortorella said. "Marty expects that and he's certainly a guy people are looking to slow down."

St. Louis' only recourse will be speed and the kind of persistence that turned an undrafted player out of the University of Vermont into a scoring champion.

"It is frustrating, but it's going to be that way and you have to fight through it," he said. "That's what I have to do."

Height: 5'9"
Weight: 181
Position: RW
Shoots: Left
Born: June 18, 1975
Laval, Quebec

St. Louis won't be alone. When referee Rob Martell refused to make a call as Odelein cross checked St. Louis in the back, center Vinny Lecavalier and defenseman Darryl Sydor rushed in to help, incurring two-minute penalties. Odelein received only a slashing minor after turning his attention to Lecavalier.

"I know a lot of my teammates, sometimes when the other teams try to frustrate me, they've got my back," St. Louis said. "And that's what I like about this team. We stand up for one another."

The same group effort will be important in establishing offense as teams try to negate the Lightning's speed and forecheck in a thicket of grabby hands. It is no secret penalties are called at a decreased rate in the playoffs.

"The penalties they should call are more the holding when the guy has the puck," Lecavalier said. "I guess they are just trying to bother Marty and get him off his game, and obviously it didn't work. I think the refs really should call the neutral zone holding and let us keep our speed, because if they don't it really slows down the game."

But they probably won't, so the Lightning must adapt.

"You just find ways to get through it," defenseman Cory Sarich said. "Dump the puck around people, keep putting yourself in that situation where you might get [a penalty call]. If you keep getting hooked down, they're going to have to call it eventually, if it's too blatant."

And until then, persist. When Odelein attempted to carry the puck out of his own end on the power play, it was St. Louis hustling to harass him at the blue line. No clutching, no grabbing, but a stick on a hurried pass and a puck that was in the Panther goal in a matter of seconds.

Now that's how you get even.

"Yeah, looking back, looking at the tape, am I happy it was [Odelein]? Yeah," St. Louis said. "He's the kind of guy who will play in your face and frustrate you. This is one way that I like to answer." —BRANT JAMES

Martin St. Louis is targeted by two Islanders, Roman Hamrlik (left) and Dave Scatchard (right), during the series with the Islanders. DIRK SHADD/ST. PETERSBURG TIMES

FREDRIK THE GREAT

BY DAMIAN CRISTODERO

Fredrik Modin sat in front of his locker and answered every question in his usual thoughtful way.

The Lightning had just scored a 3-0 victory over the Islanders in Game 1 of the East quarterfinals. And the left wing's two goals were key. But Modin would not get drawn into the hoopla.

"It's one game. We won one game," he said. "It's great, and we're very happy. But this is far, far from over. That's just the attitude we have. It's great, but we need three more."

Modin was doing more than stating the obvious. He was acknowledging not everything went Tampa Bay's way in front of a not-soldout crowd of 18,536 at the St. Pete Times Forum.

The Lightning's 18 shots were the fewest, by four, in a playoff game. The Islanders' ferocious forecheck made it difficult for Tampa Bay to get its offense going. New York even outshot Tampa Bay 15-5 in the second period.

And other than Modin, the Lightning got little offense and just nine shots from its top two lines.

But as Coach John Tortorella said, "When it comes to the playoffs, you don't overanalyze. You take your win, and you move on."

Especially when Modin and Andre Roy give you goals on two of your five second-period shots. You kill off five of five power-play situations, including three crucial ones in the game's first 11 minutes. And you get a monster game from your goaltender.

Nikolai Khabibulin, benched in the deciding Game 5 of last season's East semifinals against the Devils, brushed aside this season's doubts, not to mention the reporters who tried to talk to him afterward.

He also answered, with 30 saves, those who implied New York's Rick DiPietro, who entered

	1st	2nd	3rd	T
NY Islanders	0	0	0	0
Tampa Bay	0	2	1	3

the game with 15 minutes of playoff experience, is the better goaltender in this series.

"Nik was outstanding," Tortorella said. "That's good for Nik to play a game like that and get a win. It was tremendous for him. That was one of his better games."

He got some help. Defenseman Jassen Cullimore's skate stopped Adrian Aucoin's shot off a scramble in front of the net in the second period to preserve the 0-0 tie. And defenseman Dan Boyle stopped with his privates Michael Peca's second-period shot at an open net to keep the score 1-0.

"Hey, you need to give him credit," Islanders coach Steve Stirling said of Khabibulin. "He got a shutout. He must have been doing something right no matter how many shots we had. But you have to bury some of them."

As Roy did.

The right wing played just 4:20 on seven shifts but scored the winner, his first playoff goal, as part of a two-goal second period. Both goals came after New York defenseman Eric Cairns was stripped of the puck in the Islanders' zone.

Interesting thing about Modin. He is so well known for his big shot that many of his other assets, such as his penalty killing and forechecking ability, are missed.

That said, did you notice how his goals were scored on a backhander in front of the net and on a tip-in?

"He's going to be a very important guy in this series because of the strength [the Islanders] have

Fredrik Modin pumps his fist after scoring his second goal of the night. The Lightning shut out the Islanders 3-0 in Game 1. BILL SERNE/ST. PETERSBURG TIMES

down low with their defense as far as protecting the puck and holding onto it," Tortorella said.

Modin showed that strength with 8:54 left in the second period when he stole the puck off Cairns' stick in front of the net and sneaked it through DiPietro's legs.

He put the game away with a power-play goal with 9:01 left in the third period when he tipped in a shot from Darryl Sydor.

"I didn't have any idea I would score a couple of goals," said Modin, who had two goals in 11 previous playoff games. "I always go out there with the attitude I'm going to contribute. It was nice that I got a chance to do that.

"But there are a lot of games left. It's going to be a tough series."

The hoopla will have to wait.

KICKED IN THE GUT

DAMIAN CRISTODERO

This is how bad it got for the Lightning during Game 2 of the East quarterfinals against the Islanders. With goalie Nikolai Khabibulin pulled and playing six against five, Tampa Bay could barely break into the offensive zone.

The Islanders swarmed, passes went off target, and when the puck went to open areas, it seemed a New York player invariably got there first.

Sprinkle enough of that over 60 minutes and you get what the announced sellout crowd of 19,982 saw at the St. Pete Times Forum: the Islanders' 3-0 victory that evened the best-of-seven series at one game apiece.

"We're not battling hard enough," Lightning wing Martin St. Louis said. "Not just defensive battling, but offensive battling."

Then St. Louis dropped this bomb: "They looked hungrier."

"I agree," defenseman Dan Boyle said. "I don't know why. It's frustrating. As a player, you like to think you're giving your all. But you have to do more."

For a visual aid, Tampa Bay could look at the bench to its left.

Jason Blake, playing for the first time since sustaining a high ankle sprain on March 25, broke open a 1-0 game with two third-period goals, including an empty-netter with 55 seconds left.

Goalie Rick DiPietro, in his third playoff game, made 22 saves for his first shutout. It is up to you to decide if bumping Khabibulin after the second period as they crossed heading to their benches was accidental.

On the other hand...

Khabibulin made 22 saves, some brilliant. But during a first-period penalty kill, he let Janne Niinimaa's unobstructed shot from the blue line get through his legs.

	1st	2nd	3rd	T
NY Islanders	1	0	2	3
Tampa Bay	0	0	0	0

"I couldn't pick it up, and it went straight in," the goalie said.

The power play continues to be atrocious; 0-for-7 Saturday, 1-for-14 in the series and 5-for-55 in its past 13 games.

The top two lines are struggling (or being shut down) as New York's trap is limiting time and space. St. Louis, Vinny Lecavalier, Brad Richards, Cory Stillman and Ruslan Fedotenko were without a point for the second straight game.

And seven odd-man rushes, including semi-breakaways by St. Louis, Lecavalier and Fredrik Modin, resulted in just two shots.

When there were good chances, DiPietro, 22, stifled them. He preserved a 1-0 lead in the second period with great saves on Fedotenko's one-timer from the slot and Richards' deflection from in close.

"When he is at the top of his game, he is under control in the crease, seeing everything," Islanders coach Steve Stirling said. "Tonight, every shot, traffic or no traffic, I knew he saw the puck."

Even when it went in, it didn't count as Lecavalier's apparent goal 6:06 into the third that would have made it 2-1 was correctly disallowed because it was kicked in.

"They're a good team," Lightning coach John Tortorella said. "We've always said they're a very hard-working team that checks well. That's what's going to determine the series. Who is going to get through the checking and do the things. Tonight, we weren't able to make the big plays. [In Game 1], we were opportunistic."

The difference?

"Some guys are fighting the puck a little bit," Tortorella said. "There were a number of times when it looked like we were going to have a scoring chance and it just didn't turn into a scoring chance."

Neither Lecavalier nor Modin got shots off on their semi-breakaways, and a two-on-one fizzled when Tim Taylor's pass went into Pavel Kubina's skates.

Then there is the power play, which St. Louis called "nonexistent" and can't seem to keep the puck away from DiPietro, a stick-handling wizard and forecheck buster.

Frustrating? Tortorella scoffed.

"I believe in the hockey club," he said. "We'll be ready to play.

Being ready is one thing, Khabibulin said. "We definitely have to be more desperate."

Jassen Cullimore (5) battles Islander Alexei Yashin (79) on the ice during the third period of Game 2. The Islanders avenged the previous shutout with one of their own, 3-0. DIRK SHADD/ST. PETERSBURG TIMES

GOOD THINGS COME IN 3

DAMIAN CRISTODERO

Martin St. Louis sat in front of his locker, wiped his face with a towel and took a swig from a water bottle.

It was 20 minutes after Tampa Bay's 3-0 victory over the Islanders at the Nassau Coliseum, and St. Louis was still sweating. A shower was in order, but the Lightning wing took time to answer all questions about his team, which answered a few of its own.

"That's as desperate as I've seen us play," St. Louis said. "That's what we have to bring every game. Face every game like there's no tomorrow. It's nice to come here and do that."

So much for pressure. So much for gloom and doom. So much for the Coliseum and its loud and rowdy fans.

Tampa Bay reversed the complexion of a series in which it had been outhustled and outplayed, took a two games to one lead in the best-of-seven East quarterfinal and regained home-ice advantage.

The only bummer was the loss of defenseman Jassen Cullimore with about six minutes gone in the second period, when he and his right shoulder, the same one he hurt during the season, were crunched into the boards by Roman Hamrlik's clean check.

That will be talked about more when Cullimore is evaluated. The talk after the game was of a hustling and disciplined effort and of St. Louis' two goals, including an empty-netter with 10 seconds left.

There was Brad Richards' three points, including his first playoff goal that was part of a two-goal first period, and Nikolai Khabibulin's 28 saves for his second shutout in three games that raised his series save percentage to .976.

But there also was talk of an emotional team meeting last Sunday in which St. Louis and

	1st	2nd	3rd	T
Tampa Bay	2	0	1	**3**
NY Islanders	0	0	0	**0**

defenseman Darryl Sydor spoke and players rededicated themselves to the team's system.

Coach John Tortorella and associate coach Craig Ramsay called the meeting after the worrisome 3-0 loss, during which the Islanders clearly took the play to Tampa Bay.

"The message was pretty clear," captain Dave Andreychuk said. "We needed more effort. We needed to battle more, to seize the moment. This might not come around again."

Andreychuk said St. Louis and Sydor set the tone.

"It was all about showing one another how bad do we want it," St. Louis said. "It's not [all] out every few shifts. It's [all] out every shift. You empty the tank on every shift."

"We weren't playing playoff hockey," Sydor said. "It just opened our eyes to, 'Hey, this is it.'"

The players got the message.

"It was just kind of a reinforcement of how important it was that the desperation and effort level had to come out," Richards said.

The Islanders, pumped up by the animated crowd, were physical early. Too physical, as center Jason Blake took a bad boarding penalty which turned into Richards' power play goal 3:40 into the game, a nice confidence-builder for a unit that had gone 1-for-14 in the series.

St. Louis made it 2-0 at 6:32 and Tampa Bay held the fort through consecutive penalties thanks to a brilliant save by Khabibulin on Mark Parrish from in front of the net.

Khabibulin made 14 saves in the second and the Lightning killed off a 2:40 power play that

Brad Richards (19) celebrates after scoring the first goal of the game, en route to the third 3-0 shutout of the series, the Lightning winning two of three. DIRK SHADD/ST. PETERSBURG TIMES

included 1:20 of four-on-three. The third period was all Tampa Bay, which held the Islanders to five shots.

"They did a good job in the neutral zone," Islanders coach Steve Stirling said. "I think we were a half-step late and they had some jump. They did a good job and we didn't help ourselves."

"I think we needed to get out of the gear of the regular season and play playoff intensity," Tortorella said. "You can rip apart a series and go through all the line changes, it eventually comes back to being a simple game. Who's going to compete? Who's going to win certain battles at key times of the games?"

On this time it was the Lightning.

Goaltender Nikolai Khabibulin earned his second shutout in three games, the only ones in Lightning playoff history.

Center Brad Richards celebrates after beating goalie Rick DiPietro for a goal, his first in 14 career playoff games, to put the Lightning ahead 1-0 3:40 into the game on a power play.

NOTHIN' GETS BY NIK

DAMIAN CRISTODERO

As the Lightning skated to the locker room after the game at the Nassau Coliseum, crumpled paper began littering the ice.

An empty beer bottle skidded to a stop in the Tampa Bay zone. Some of the rally towels given to Islanders fans before the game either made it to the ice or hit the surrounding glass.

Somewhere, there was a chant of "Let's go Yankees."

For the Lightning, after a 3-0 victory in Game 4 of the East quarterfinals, the derision was confirmation of a job well done.

"It shows we got their team frustrated and their fans," defenseman Dan Boyle said. "They feed off that crowd.

That New York's fans were upset was understandable. Tampa Bay took a three games to one lead in the best-of-seven series and has a chance to clinch in Game 5 at the St. Pete Times Forum.

But their anger was misplaced. More notable than what the Islanders did not do was what the Lightning did. In front of a hostile crowd and playing against a motivated opponent who wanted nothing less than to fall two games behind in the series, Tampa Bay withstood the onslaught.

It did it despite the loss to injury of defenseman Jassen Cullimore and wing Cory Stillman, who left the game after one shift with what the team described as a lower-body injury. He was seen on the bench icing his left hip.

"It's unbelievable," Richards said. "We could have come in here, and it would have been easy to tighten the grip on your stick. But we stayed focused and looked straight ahead and made big plays when we needed them."

	1st	2nd	3rd	T
Tampa Bay	1	1	1	3
NY Islanders	0	0	0	0

Big plays such as Martin St. Louis' exquisite short-handed goal in the first period. Richards' perfect pass that set up Ruslan Fedotenko's second-period goal. And the third-period blast from Fredrik Modin that Islanders goalie Rick DiPietro has yet to see.

St. Louis and Modin also had assists. Richards had two. And then there was Nikolai Khabibulin.

Is there anything left to say? His 33 saves gave him a third shutout and improved his save percentage to .983 with 113 saves on 115 shots.

But there was more to Tampa Bay's victory than stats. More than any game this season, this one offered proof of how the team has grown.

The Islanders came out roaring, and Khabibulin was there. New York had the game's first two power plays, yet St. Louis scored the goal.

The Islanders surged in the second period, but Fedotenko deflated them with his goal with 1:57 left on a two-on-one that began with Modin's block at the Lightning blue line of Adrian Aucoin's slap shot.

"Maturity, determination, all of those things," defenseman Cory Sarich said. "Just believing in ourselves. All those things go into the mix."

"Our team is maturing," Coach John Tortorella said. "I think it has quite a bit more maturing to do, but we found a way. In the playoffs, you just look to find a way. You try to win the battles. You try to keep it simple, especially in the situation we came in here."

So you clog the middle of the ice to defuse a 33-20 shot disadvantage. You chip the puck out of the defensive zone when you can to disrupt the offensive flow.

You kill a crucial short-handed situation with 4:46 left in the second period and the score 1-0. And when all else fails, you rely on your goaltender.

Khabibulin's sharp right-leg save through traffic of Aucoin's slap shot 6:55 into the game set

a tone, as did the goalie's stop of Aucoin's one-timer in the slot with 7:25 left.

Captain Dave Andreychuk was on the spot in the second period when he smacked the puck out of the slot moments before New York's Oleg Kvasha could shoot at a half-open net after a Khabibulin save.

The boos?

"They pay [for tickets]. They can do what they want," DiPietro said. "I'm sure Tampa feeds off that when the whole crowd boos like that."

For the Lightning, it's all part of growing up.

Brad Lukowich (right) and Michael Peca (left) fight for control of the puck during second-period action in Game 4. The Lightning shut out the Islanders 3-0 for the third time in the series. DIRK SHADD/ST. PETERSBURG TIMES

ECSTASY IN OVERTIME

DAMIAN CRISTODERO

Things are not always as they seem when it comes to shooting a puck.

Conventional wisdom says players want it lying flat on the ice. It certainly is easier to give it a whack. But funny things can happen when you shoot a puck that sits on its edge, and that is exactly what Martin St. Louis was counting on.

"It's tough to stop a puck that's rolling," the Lightning wing said later in the quiet of the locker room. "I was lucky I got good wood on it."

Luck had nothing to do with the shot that gave Tampa Bay a 3-2 overtime victory over the Islanders in Game 5 of the East quarterfinals and sent the Lightning to the second round of the playoffs.

It was supersonic and pinpoint accurate into a corner of the net over the glove of New York goaltender Rick DiPietro 4:07 into the extra session.

St. Louis' fourth goal of the playoffs gave the top-seeded Lightning a four games to one win in the best-of-seven series, and the team avoided going back to Long Island for a dreaded Game 6.

Most fun, though, it sent the sellout crowd of 20,927, the third largest at the St. Pete Times Forum, into a roof-raising frenzy.

"He's our guy," defenseman Brad Lukowich said of St. Louis. "He's just our guy. It doesn't surprise me that he can do things like that. It doesn't surprise me at all."

"Man, the MVP came through, didn't he?" center Tim Taylor said. "You look for heroes and MVPs, and his name keeps jumping out.

"Obviously, his body keeps jumping out, too."

It was the second straight season St. Louis propelled the Lightning into the conference semifinals. Last season, it was with a goal in the third overtime of Game 6 against the Capitals.

	1st	2nd	3rd	OT	T
NY Islanders	1	0	1	0	2
Tampa Bay	0	2	0	1	3

Just like last season, he had help.

Lightning goaltender Nikolai Khabibulin had his shutout streak stopped at two and at 145:09 when Oleg Kvasha scored 10:41 into the first period to give New York a 1-0 lead. But Khabibulin made 24 saves to finish the series with 137 on 141 shots for a .972 save percentage.

Fredrik Modin was huge with three assists. And Taylor and Ruslan Fedotenko scored in a stretch of 2:04 of the second period to turn a 1-0 deficit into a 2-1 lead with 1:38 remaining.

The Islanders tied the score 7:28 into the third period when Mark Parrish tipped in Janne Niinimaa's shot from the point. But all that did was set up St. Louis' big finish.

"You don't want to write it up that way," Coach John Tortorella said. "You don't want to give up the lead in the third period and allow them to tie. But to win in overtime is pretty exciting. That's good stuff.

"And Marty, rightly so. He has the heart of a lion."

"It's right up there, obviously," St. Louis said of where the goal ranks in his career. "I'm called upon for a lot of offense, and I try my best to help my team win. But whoever would have scored I would have been happy."

The game had its unconventional side as well.

It was the first of the series that did not end 3-0, meaning it joins the 1993 division final between the Canadiens and Sabres as the only ones to start a series with four identical scores.

There also were two video reviews. Kvasha's goal was scored at with 9:19 but not acknowl-

Islanders goaltender Rick DiPietro (39) looks back to see the puck in the net after the Lightning's second goal. The Lightning won the game and the series in overtime. (DIRK SHADD/ST. PETERSBURG TIMES)

edged until 2:12 later when a stoppage of play finally allowed a review.

It looked as if Brad Richards tied the score with 7:47 remaining when referee Don Koharski signaled the center's redirect had sneaked past DiPietro. But that also was correctly reversed.

Tortorella said the Lightning knew both calls would go against them, so the bench did not get down.

It was up in the second period as Tampa Bay took over the game, outshooting the Islanders 15-5 and getting the lead when Taylor scored his first playoff goal in 60 games after Modin's end-to-end rush and Fedotenko whacked in a rebound of a Modin shot.

ROUND 2

Lightning

Sweep

Canadiens, 4-0

The Lightning celebrate the second-round sweep of the Canadiens at the Bell Centre in Montreal.
DAN MCDUFFIE/ST. PETERSBURG TIMES

A ROUT, EH? LIGHTNING SKATE TO EASY WIN

DAMIAN CRISTODERO

Lightning wing Martin St. Louis said it was no big deal.

He and center Vinny Lecavalier played on the same line since January. That they are back together after a two-week break during the East quarterfinals shouldn't be a shock.

But in the aftermath of Tampa Bay's resounding 4-0 victory over the Canadiens in Game 1 of the East semifinals at the St. Pete Times Forum, it was just about all anybody could talk about.

Lecavalier had two goals and an assist. St. Louis had three assists. For good measure, linemate Ruslan Fedotenko had a goal.

And all seemed right with the world, though St. Louis wasn't convinced.

"You're making more out of it than it really is," he said. "It's not like we're finding each other again. We're good players, and we feed off each

	1st	2nd	3rd	T
Montreal	0	0	0	**0**
Tampa Bay	0	2	2	**4**

Vincent Lecavalier rejoices after scoring his second goal of the game against Montreal. The Lightning shut out the Canadiens 4-0 in Game 1. DAN MCDUFFIE/ST. PETERSBURG TIMES

other. It's not like Vinny doesn't know my game, and it's not like I don't know his."

What we do know is one of the best story lines of this series has begun to take shape.

Hats off to goalie Nikolai Khabibulin, who made 21 saves for his fourth playoff shutout after getting just three in the regular season. Kudos to the defense that blocked a ton of shots and made sure that most of what got through came from the outside.

And good for Dmitry Afanasenkov, who got his first playoff goal 7:20 into the third period. That was a little more than three minutes after Lecavalier's second goal and chased Canadiens goalie Jose Theodore in favor of Mathieu Garon after Theodore allowed four goals on 28 shots.

But it is the Lecavalier-St. Louis connection that is so engaging. Both grew up in the suburbs of Montreal idolizing the Canadiens; St. Louis in Laval and Lecavalier in Ile-Bizard.

Don't think there isn't pressure to perform.

St. Louis' comes from a regular season in which he led the league with 94 points. Lecavalier's from the fact he had zero points against the Islanders in the quarterfinals and just one point, an assist, in his previous 10 playoff games.

In that sense, misery loves company. And that company includes Fedotenko, a good skater who gives the line another dimension with his willingness to get to the net.

Lightning center Vincent Lecavalier scores against Canadien goaltender Jose Theodore in the second period. DIRK SHADD/ST. PETERSBURG TIMES

"We do click together," Lecavalier said. "We knew how important this game was. It was huge to get that first win."

But if things are so good, why was the line separated for the Islanders series when Cory

Stillman was with Lecavalier and Fedotenko and St. Louis took Stillman's spot with center Brad Richards and Fredrik Modin?

"No matter what line you have, at some point, you separate people and put them back together," associate coach Craig Ramsay said. "What it does is it builds up a little excitement again. 'Hey, we're back together. This is fun.'

"You get a little complacent sometimes. You're going through the year playing together. Sometimes you stop really talking and really communicating. And then tossed back together and it's exciting and then you push."

Such as the way Lecavalier pushed for the puck along the side boards in the Canadiens' zone and outworked Montreal's Mike Ribeiro. St. Louis grabbed the puck and passed to Fedotenko, who opened the scoring 2:52 into the second period from the slot.

Lecavalier made it 2-0 with 3:17 left in the period when he tipped in St. Louis' shot.

The game was a huge disappointment to the Canadiens, who repeatedly said they could not afford a start such as the one that helped get them into a three games to one hole against the Bruins.

But Tampa Bay dominated the first period and at one point held a 7-0 shot advantage en route to a 34-21 edge in the game, the fewest shots Tampa Bay has allowed in a home playoff game.

"We thought we had our lesson that [Friday] would have been different," Theodore said. "We didn't play the way we should."

"We beat ourselves," defenseman Craig Rivet said. "There's no doubt about it. There's no other way to look at it."

Unless you look at St. Louis and Lecavalier, though St. Louis still wasn't buying.

"It doesn't matter what me and Vinny did," he said. "The bottom line is we got the win. That's the most important thing."

And a very big deal indeed.

Fans show their support at the St. Pete Times Forum. DAN MCDUFFIE/ST. PETERSBURG TIMES

VINNY STRIKES TWICE

DAMIAN CRISTODERO

He hesitated, made a face and shrugged his shoulders. Nikolai Khabibulin believed he was on dangerous ground. Better, then, not to say too much.

The Lightning goalie never has enjoyed explaining how or why he plays well or poorly. And with Khabibulin in a zone reserved for a special few, the discomfort has increased.

He admitted as much after the 3-1 victory over the Canadiens in Game 2 of the East semifinals at the St. Pete Times Forum.

So after offering, "I'm trying to do the same things" and "I didn't try to do anything different," Khabibulin said he didn't want to jinx anything, especially with a two games to none lead in the best-of-seven series.

	1st	2nd	3rd	T
Montreal	1	0	0	1
Tampa Bay	2	1	0	3

"I guess," he said, "it's a little bit of that, too."

Which left it to Khabibulin's teammates to exult over his 26-save effort that included an 11-save second period in which the surging Canadiens outplayed Tampa Bay but could not close a 2-1 deficit.

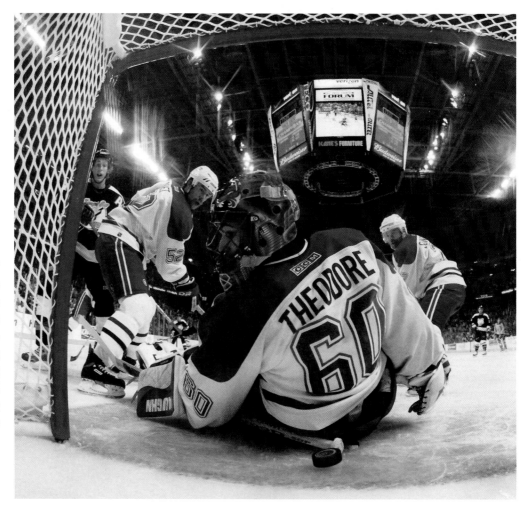

Canadiens goaltender Jose Theodore looks over his shoulder to see the puck crossing the goal line on a first-period shot by Vincent Lecavalier. The Lightning held on to the lead and beat Montreal 3-1. DIRK SHADD/ST. PETERSBURG TIMES

Canadien Andrei Markov skates past as the Lightning celebrate the second goal of the game, scored by Fredrik Modin. DIRK SHADD/ST. PETERSBURG TIMES

Vinny Lecavalier's second goal of the game and fourth of the series, on a breakaway with 2.4 seconds left in the period after a bad giveaway by Montreal defenseman Sheldon Souray, was the payoff.

But it also spotlighted the importance of Khabibulin holding off Montreal, which outshot Tampa Bay 11-8 in the period.

"He was unbelievable," defenseman Pavel Kubina said. "He made some great saves. He's

A second goal from Vincent Lecavalier is cause for celebration in the second period. BILL SERNE/ST. PETERSBURG TIMES

been great the whole playoffs. It's just amazing to watch him in the net with what he's capable of."

"He made huge stops," defenseman Cory Sarich said. "Strong, strong again."

It is an old story in these playoffs, but one that keeps getting better.

Khabibulin has stopped 184 of 189 shots for a .974 save percentage in his six victories. He came within one save of his fifth shutout. But after stopping Alex Kovalev's point shot and Saku Koivu's rebound attempt, Koivu's second rebound shot went over the sprawling goaltender.

The power-play goal with 3:20 left in the first cut a two-goal deficit produced by Lecavalier's five-on-three goal 2:35 into the game and Fredrik Modin's goal at 8:33.

Tampa Bay had a 10-0 advantage in shots at that point. But from then through the end of the second, the Lightning got sloppy, especially in the neutral zone, and were outshot 19-11 but, thanks to Khabibulin, not outdone.

Khabibulin shone on a Montreal power play with a terrific right-leg save on Michael Ryder's blast from the high slot with 8:49 left in the second. Twenty seconds later, he stopped Yanic Perreault's redirection in front of the net. He stopped Kovalev's breakaway with 5:25 left.

"We knew they were doing some good things in that period. It's just a matter of getting through it without getting scarred," Lightning coach John Tortorella said. "Your goaltender has to be good, and Nik was excellent at that point in time."

And Lecavalier provided the back breaker on a goal that began innocently with Souray's giveaway as he approached Tampa Bay's blue line. Sarich's blind, off-the-boards pass was right on the stick of the center, who broke the other way as soon as Sarich gained the puck.

"I didn't even know Vinny was there," Sarich said. "I knew they had three guys coming up, so I was just getting it out of there."

"When you leave a player like Lecavalier behind the play, it becomes dangerous," Canadiens coach Claude Julien said. "We made sure everybody was in front of us, but we got caught flat-footed."

And the Lightning are off and running as they prepare for Game 3 at the Bell Centre.

"It was important to win the two games here," Khabibulin said. "But at the same time, we haven't done anything yet. We know going to Montreal, it's going to be a crazy place, and they are going to play a lot better."

"I think they will be a better team," Tortorella said. "I think both teams will be better."

And the Lightning won't be jinxed.

NEVER SAY NEVER

DAMIAN CRISTODERO

The first thing Glen Richards did was call his wife, Delite. It wasn't so much a conversation as a series of screams and yelps.

Their son, Brad, had just scored his second goal 65 seconds into overtime to give the Lightning a 4-3 victory over the Canadiens at the Bell Centre. And Glen, who had flown in that morning from Prince Edward Island, just couldn't believe his luck. Or was that Brad's skill?

	1st	2nd	3rd	OT	T
Tampa Bay	0	2	1	1	**4**
Montreal	0	1	2	0	**3**

Lobster season begins this Friday, and Glen and Delite will be manning the boats. That is why Delite could not make it. That is why that game could be the only playoff game this season Glen will see his son play.

Vincent Lecavalier beats Montreal Canadiens goaltender Jose Theodore to tie the score, 3-3, during the final seconds of the third period. Tampa Bay won the game in overtime, 4-3. DIRK SHADD/ST. PETERSBURG TIMES

Canadien Andrei Markov hits the ice early in Game 3 as Lecavalier tries for control of the puck.
DIRK SHADD/ST. PETERSBURG TIMES

"It was unbelievable," Glen said. "You couldn't have written it any better. Awesome. And how dramatic it was."

"Unbelievable," Brad said. "The best feeling in life. You wish you could do it over and over again. It was just so much fun. It was unbelievable."

Believe this. With the victory in Game 3 of the East semifinals, the Lightning's sixth consecutive of the playoffs, they are one win from a sweep in the best-of-seven series and a spot in the East final.

As if Richards' goal wasn't enough to set hearts pounding—he purposely banked his own rebound off the left skate of goalie Jose Theodore—consider the Lightning were 16.5 seconds from a 3-2 loss that would have cut Montreal's deficit to two games to one and changed the dynamic of the series.

But Vinny Lecavalier's spectacular goal, his fifth of the series, in which he redirected Dave Andreychuk's cross-slot pass through his legs (that's right, through his legs) and past Theodore, tied the score.

And then there was Nikolai Khabibulin. The goalie allowed three goals, his playoff high. But none were his fault, and he was brilliant while making 28 saves.

"We got her done," wing Martin St. Louis said. "That's character. No matter how well or bad we played, we got her done."

In a pressure cooker.

The sellout crowd of 21,273 was louder than many Lightning players said they had ever heard, and it booed hometowners Lecavalier, St. Louis and Eric Perrin. The Canadiens also turned mean.

Twenty-one penalties for 58 minutes were called, including 17 for 34 minutes in the first. Face washes, cross-checks and good, hard checks were everywhere. Even the 5-foot-8, 176-pound Perrin got into a wrestling match with 6 foot 4, 237-pound Mike Komisarek.

Cory Stillman's first goal of the playoffs, on a short-handed breakaway, and Richards' power-play tally gave the Lightning a 2-1 second-period lead. But Michael Ryder and Patrice Brisebois scored in the third to give Montreal a 3-2 edge with 3:47 left.

It was clear, Montreal, which outshot Tampa Bay 31-28, was forcing the action.

"When you score three goals in playoff hockey, it should be enough to win," said Canadiens wing Alex Kovalev, who scored in the second period. "All we can do now is relax. You can play like a kid."

And as determined as Tampa Bay did after Montreal took the lead.

"We stayed together," Lightning coach John Tortorella said. "I think the most important thing in playoff hockey is handling those type of situations. We still had time."

Lecavalier's goal had all kinds of subplots. A faceoff victory by Andreychuk, who lost a faceoff on Brisebois' goal. A great play by defenseman Pavel Kubina to keep the puck in the offensive zone and poke it to St. Louis.

And a remarkable flick of Lecavalier's stick. "Fancy was the only option," he said.

Richards' winner wasn't fancy. It was calculated.

"The puck came right back to me so quickly, and you could see he didn't know where it was," he said of Theodore. "I just tried to bank it off him. I was happy it went in."

"A spectacular play," Glen Richards said. "My wife was screaming. It was unbelievable."

It was the least Brad could do. He likely won't be around for lobster season.

The Lightning celebrate Brad Richards' game-winning overtime goal to give Tampa Bay a 3-0 series lead. DAN MCDUFFIE/ST. PETERSBURG TIMES

LIGHTNING MAKE HISTORY WITH CANADIEN SWEEP

DAMIAN CRISTODERO

So much for enjoying the moment. So much for savoring the biggest victory in team history.

Defenseman Dan Boyle sat in the locker room after the Lightning's 3-1 win over the Canadiens gave them a sweep of the East semifinals and declared, "We're not done. We're not going to be satisfied getting to the third round."

	1st	2nd	3rd	T
Tampa Bay	0	2	1	**3**
Montreal	1	0	0	**1**

Brad Richards scores the Lightning's second goal against Montreal's goaltender, Jose Theodore, during the second period. The Lightning swept the series with the win. DIRK SHADD/ST. PETERSBURG TIMES

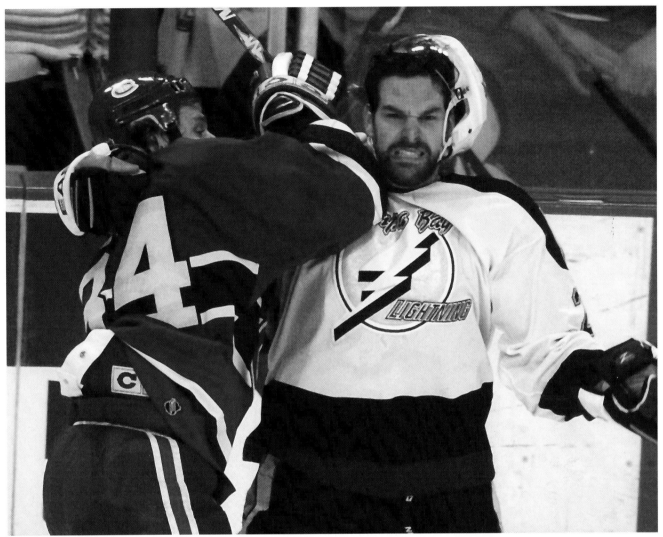

Tampa Bay's Dan Boyle and Montreal's Jim Dowd trade blows during third-period action. DIRK SHADD/ST. PETERSBURG TIMES

It was not long ago, just two seasons in fact, when it was satisfying enough for Tampa Bay to not have the word "lowly" automatically connected to its name. That almost is quaint after what the team accomplished at the Bell Centre.

The Lightning didn't just advance to the conference final for the first time in the team's 12-season history—and, oh, by the way, they will be thrilled if the Flyers and Maple Leafs beat each other's brains out for seven games—they earned a piece of history.

Only three previous times had the Canadiens, winners of a record 24 Stanley Cups, been swept in a seven-game series. Only once, in the 1998 East final against the Sabres, had they lost the fourth game at home.

It was an added kick.

"It's not the players. It's the history and tradition you're proud to play against," center Brad Richards said. "It's special to play against the uniform and its history."

That aside, Richards said of the victory, "It's incredible. There has never been anything bigger. We wanted to take care of business. There's never any other feeling when you win. It's great."

Dan Boyle (22) is surrounded by teammates Vincent Lecavalier, Dave Andreychuk, Brad Richards, and Martin St. Louis following a goal in the second period. AP/WWP

Which is how Richards should feel. After scoring the winner in Game 3, he got another in Game 4 with 2:46 left in the second as part of a two-goal period that overcame a 1-0 deficit.

Boyle scored on the power play. Fredrik Modin's empty-net goal capped it with 55.3 seconds left in the third period, and Dave Andreychuk and Dmitry Afanasenkov had two assists each.

raise his save percentage to .964. He allowed five goals in the series.

He had a little luck. Richard Zednik hit the crossbar with 56.2 seconds left in the first period. And Sheldon Souray's screaming second-period slap shot trickled past Khabibulin and settled against the outside of the post before he covered up.

"We just didn't get the results," Zednik said. "It's not the way you want to lose. Right now, I don't have too many positive things in my mind."

It was all positive as the game started. The sellout crowd of 21,273 was deafening (even without ThunderStix) and was primed by the pregame ceremony that celebrated the team's history.

It was madness when Sundstrom scored 5:46 into the first period after Boyle gave up the puck in the Lightning zone when he said he hit a rut in the ice and fell.

The players said they laughed off the miscue.

"It was early," said Brad Lukowich, Boyle's defensive partner. "If you're going to let that bother you, it's going to be an ugly night. There was tons of time in front of us. If you worry about it, you're going to make more mistakes."

"It comes down to intensity and battling," Coach John Tortorella said. "If you understand that and raise it as you go through and win those battles, that's what's most important. This year, we elevated in the second round more so than the first."

Boyle evened the score with 8:03 left in the second period when Vinny Lecavalier's pass deflected sharply off Boyle's shin guard and past goalie Jose Theodore.

Richards scored his third goal in two games by roofing a backhander over Theodore after Afanasenkov picked off Jim Dowd's blind drop pass in the Lightning zone and transitioned the other way.

"It feels great," Afanasenkov said. "A big goal for us."

But not the biggest.

"We have our sights set on going all the way," Boyle said.

"We're halfway there."

What else can be said about Nikolai Khabibulin, who led the team to its seventh consecutive victory? The goalie made 27 saves, 26 after Niklas Sundstrom's early first-period goal, to

#35 NIKOLAI KHABIBULIN

While the English-speaking reporters waited patiently, Montreal coach Claude Julien described in his native French how his team was swept out of the playoffs by the Lightning. What, Claude, was the difference?

On and on he went for nearly a minute until finally he hit a word that everyone in the room understood. Oddly enough, the word was neither French or English. It was Russian.

Khabibulin.

Once upon a time—oh, like a few weeks ago—Lightning goalie Nikolai Khabibulin had a reputation of being about as reliable as a '75 Pinto in the playoffs. Start, sputter, stop. Bad goal here, bad goal there and a quick detour off the first exit ramp of the postseason.

Before this season, Khabibulin was 15-18 in the playoffs. He had lost two Game 7s. He was yanked in last year's series against New Jersey. He had won one series in five tries.

In the past three weeks, he has won two. He has gone from a beat-up Pinto to a steady thoroughbred. Well, that's what the Lightning say.

"They always say you've got to ride a hot goalie until the end," Lightning defenseman Dan Boyle said. "That's what we're going to do. He stole some games in the first round. And he definitely came up big the last two games in Montreal. He's our horse right now."

He is what goalies call being "in the zone," or "in the groove." It's what the Lightning call "in the conference finals."

Khabibulin stopped 27 of 28 shots in Game 4. He stopped 102 of 107 in the series.

Height: 6'1"
Weight: 203
Position: G
Catches: Left
Born: January 13, 1973
Sverdlovsk, USSR

"I think without him, we're not even in this series," Boyle said. "You know he is going to make the big stop."

The big stop. The small stops. Pretty much every stop.

He has faced 248 shots in this postseason. Only nine have found the net.

Most important, he is 8-1.

"Nik has been our best player," Lightning coach John Tortorella said. "He has been our best player, and he is going to have to be our best player if we're going to move on in this thing."

Throughout these playoffs, Khabibulin has been as difficult to solve off the ice as he has been on. Quiet and reserved, he rarely has much to say on the few occasions he has talked to the media. Most days, he ducks reporters by sneaking out a back door. It's not that he is being rude as much as he can't dissect what he's doing other than seeing the puck and stopping the puck.

He really did appear to think of an answer when asked if he has ever played better in his life, but he just shrugged his shoulders and said, "I don't really think about it. I guess whatever happens, happens."

What has happened is Khabibulin playing his best. After all, he has never carried a team this far.

"Nik Khabibulin has been the backbone of this team," Tortorella said.

Khabibulin just keeps on talking softly and carrying a big goalie's stick.

"I'm just trying to go out and stop shots," Khabibulin said. "I don't think I'm doing anything special."

But 8-1? Nine goals in eight games? That sounds special. In any language. —TOM JONES

Solid goaltender Nikolai Khabibulin stops a shot by Flyers player Branko Radivojevic. DIRK SHADD/ST. PETERSBURG TIMES

ROUND 3

Lightning Beat Flyers, 4-3

Tampa Bay celebrates a goal by Ruslan Fedotenko during the first period against the Philadelphia Flyers in Game 7 of the third round of the Stanley Cup playoffs. DIRK SHADD/ST. PETERSBURG TIMES

ONE DOWN

DAMIAN CRISTODERO

Who knew hockey players read their press clippings so closely? And who knew they could have such an effect?

In the end, it was just a vainglorious blip in what turned into a good beginning for the Lightning against the Flyers in the East final. And the 3-1 victory in Game 1 in front of a screaming sellout crowd of 21,425, the largest ever at the St.

	1st	2nd	3rd	T
Philadelphia	0	1	0	**1**
Tampa Bay	0	2	1	**3**

Pete Times Forum, looked just fine on the scoreboard.

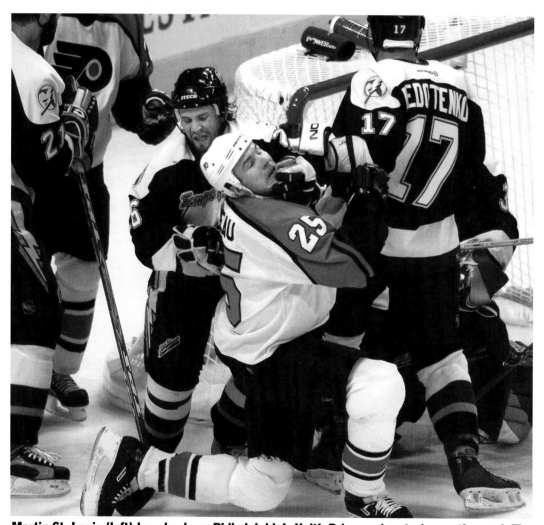

Martin St. Louis (left) knocks down Philadelphia's Keith Primeau (center) near the goal. The Lightning allowed only one goal en route to a Game 1 victory. DOUGLAS R. CLIFFORD/ST. PETERSBURG TIMES

Lightning goaltender Nikolai Khabibulin fights the Flyers' Keith Primeau for an early save. Khabibulin made nine saves in the first period. DIRK SHADD/ST. PETERSBURG TIMES

Still, there was that first period. The Flyers looked strong, the Lightning rusty. And while center Tim Taylor said some of that was attributable to an eight-day layoff after sweeping the Canadiens in the semifinals, he admitted the team might have been a bit full of itself as well.

"All we read about was how fast we are and how great a team we are and how we were going to burn them with our speed," Taylor said. "You start thinking, 'Maybe we are that great.'"

"Absolutely," right wing Martin St. Louis said. "You read that stuff, and after a while, mentally, maybe you're not as sharp."

The Lightning, then, need to send a huge thank-you smooch to goalie Nikolai Khabibulin, who made nine saves in the first period as Philadelphia came in waves and held a 9-5 shot advantage but couldn't break a 0-0 tie.

Lightning captain Dave Andreychuk got his first playoff goal and center Brad Richards his fifth

Philadelphia goaltender Robert Esche loses his footing after a goal by Tampa Bay's Chris Dingman in the third period. DOUGLAS R. CLIFFORD/ST. PETERSBURG TIMES

in the second period for a 2-1 lead. And Chris Dingman scored a huge goal 7:04 into the third with assists from fourth-line mates Eric Perrin and Andre Roy.

Cory Stillman and Fredrik Modin had two assists each, and Khabibulin made 19 saves for his and Tampa Bay's eighth consecutive victory.

"I thought our guys handled themselves very well in getting settled," Lightning coach John Tortorella said. "I thought both teams grinded. It was a battle around both nets, and both teams played very well around their nets."

Tampa Bay was exceptional there in the final 2:02 after Stillman was called for tripping. It allowed one shot on the power play and none in the final 1:42 after goalie Robert Esche was pulled and Philadelphia played six-on-four.

In fact, the Lightning allowed only 11 shots in the final two periods, including Michal Handzus' goal 6:48 into the second on a rebound after Khabibulin stopped a sharp deflection off Handzus' skate.

But that was the only crack in an escalating defensive effort that came together after the forwards decided to get involved, something that didn't happen in the first period.

"And they caught us," Taylor said of the Flyers. "They're a good team. And we just weren't helping our D. That gave them a lot of opportunities."

"We didn't come in here by any stretch of the imagination assuming to go [only] four games, and I don't think they did either," Esche said. "We're excited about playing the next game on Monday, and that's the way you have to look at it. I don't think anybody is happy about losing the first game, but you can't get too high or too low at any point in the series."

Philadelphia was on a high when it appeared Sami Kapanen scored on a rebound 6:02 into the game after Khabibulin stopped Keith Primeau's breakaway. But the goal was waved off, and Primeau, who fell into Khabibulin, was called for goaltender interference.

Tampa Bay got more help from referee Dan Marouelli, whose butt deflected Kim Johnsson's clearing attempt to Stillman, who started the sequence that led to Andreychuk's goal 2:03 into the second.

Stillman's interception in the Flyers zone of Mark Recchi's pass led to Richards' goal with 6:26 left.

And Dingman apparently did well in high school geometry as his angled pass off the boards for Roy created the shot that rebounded to Dingman for his goal.

"We had a pretty good team effort," Khabibulin said. "But we know they're going to play better the next game, so we have to play better, too."

And stay away from the newspapers. Who knew?

"Check the bathroom," Taylor said. "They're all in there."

FLYERS ZAP LIGHTNING WINNING STREAK

DAMIAN CRISTODERO

Lightning players had said it since they won Game 1 of the East final against the Flyers, but wing Martin St. Louis expressed it best.

"They're going to be a lot better," he said of Philadelphia. "They're going to be a lot better offensively. Better all around."

And the Lightning were worse. It added up to an awful 6-2 loss to the Flyers in Game 2 at the St. Pete Times Forum.

The losing margin tied Tampa Bay's worst of the season.

Philadelphia scored three times on five shots in the game's first 11:17. John LeClair got his first goal of the playoffs 1:53 in. Mark Recchi also scored, and Sami Kapanen scored short-handed.

That the Lightning finally lost was no surprise. The team had won eight straight, tying a franchise record, since losing Game 2 of the quarterfinals to the Islanders. But the game was more of a stinker than expected.

Nikolai Khabibulin, who entered the game with a playoffs-low 1.00 goals-against average, allowed two bad goals. The last—Vladimir Malakhov's first playoff goal on a simple wrist shot from the point that beat Khabibulin short side 6:02 into the second—got him pulled.

Khabibulin allowed four goals on 12 shots. John Grahame, who had not played since a victory over the Panthers on April 1, made 17 saves in relief.

Defenseman Marcus Ragnarsson had three assists for the Flyers. Michal Handzus and Mattias Timander also scored, and goalie Robert Esche made 29 saves.

	1st	2nd	3rd	T
Philadelphia	3	2	1	6
Tampa Bay	0	0	2	2

Ruslan Fedotenko and St. Louis scored for Tampa Bay in the third after the score was 6-0.

Things got rough with 12:30 left in the third. A scrum led to a fight between Tampa Bay defenseman Darryl Sydor and Danny Markov. Lightning wing Andre Roy intervened after Markov got on top of Sydor and kept punching. Roy was confronted by Branko Radivojevic.

Roy received a roughing penalty and a game misconduct. Lightning defenseman Pavel Kubina was called for high-sticking and roughing and a 10-minute misconduct.

The upshot of the 48 minutes in penalties was a four-minute five-on-three for the Flyers, which went nowhere. In another melee with 8:53 left that included a fight between Tampa Bay's Chris Dingman and Donald Brashear, the Flyers received, in a questionable bit of officiating, a four-minute power play, including two minutes of five-on-three.

You had a sense something was up in the first when the Flyers took a 1-0 lead 1:53 into the period.

LeClair, who had zero goals and an assist in the playoffs, charged into the Lightning zone and picked up the puck on the left wing. His shot, the Flyers' first of the game, from the bottom half of the faceoff circle stayed low and slipped through Khabibulin's legs. It was the 11th goal Khabibulin had allowed in 11 playoff games and the first for which he was at fault.

It appeared the Lightning were gaining some momentum from what looked like a solid penalty kill that after 1:23 of five-on-four went to five-on-three for 37 seconds.

Tampa Bay did not allow a shot in that sequence. But with the teams back to five-on-four, Recchi tipped in Ragnarsson's shot/pass from the point. Recchi was left completely alone. His tip from the hash marks was perfect, and the Flyers had a 2-0 lead at 8:50.

Tampa Bay called a timeout to settle itself. It didn't help on an ensuing power play. The Lightning continued to struggle with the extra skater and this time gave up a short-handed goal to Kapanen with 8:43 remaining.

Everything went wrong. First, the puck hit Tampa Bay defenseman Dan Boyle, who was leaving the ice. Timander picked it up and flipped the puck past Kubina at the blue line, which created a two-on-one. Kapanen skated at Khabibulin and roofed a shot from in close.

Flyers Michal Handzus (26) scores on Lightning goalie John Grahame in the third period of Game 2. The Flyers won the game 6-2 and tied the series. DIRK SHADD/ST. PETERSBURG TIMES

LIGHTNING PROVE IT'S NOT ALL TALK

DAMIAN CRISTODERO

Dan Boyle didn't know how to explain it. But the Lightning defenseman said he had a feeling before the game against the Flyers.

Was it prescience or, as Boyle called it, "a vibe," a "sixth sense"?

	1st	2nd	3rd	T
Tampa Bay	2	0	2	**4**
Philadelphia	0	0	1	**1**

Flyers goaltender Robert Esche is unable to make the save on a third-period shot by Vincent Lecavalier. The Lightning scored one more goal to win the game 4-1. DIRK SHADD/ST. PETERSBURG TIMES

Whatever, he said, "I was feeling good about how things were going to go."

Feeling good at the start turned into feeling great at the end as Tampa Bay earned a 4-1 victory and silenced an orange-clad sellout crowd of 19,987 at the Wachovia Center.

The Lightning have a two games to one lead in the best-of-seven series and regained home-ice advantage. They also are 8-0 when scoring first and remained the only playoff team undefeated on the road at 5-0.

But that was just window dressing in the team's most impressive win of the season. Not only did it come just three days after the Flyers smoked the Lightning 6-2 in Game 2, it came amid speculation the team was overmatched against a speedy and rugged Philadelphia team that had been unbeaten at home during the playoffs.

Brad Richards celebrates his goal with Martin St. Louis, who picked up an assist.
DIRK SHADD/ST. PETERSBURG TIMES

"A lot of people are probably surprised," center Brad Richards said. "We're not. We know what we can do. It's a great win. Right now, it feels unbelievable."

"What we did," wing Martin St. Louis said, "was a big character win."

Tampa Bay got first-period goals from Cory Stillman and Ruslan Fedotenko and third-period goals from Vinny Lecavalier and Richards.

Richards also had an assist. St. Louis had two in the third period. Goalie Nikolai Khabibulin made 24 saves, and Darryl Sydor was huge on defense.

And special mention to defenseman Stan Neckar, who was solid filling in for the injured Brad Lukowich in his first game since being acquired from the Predators at the trade deadline.

The only blip came 36 seconds into the third period, when Flyers captain Keith Primeau, a force throughout, cut Philadelphia's deficit to 2-1. Lecavalier restored order 43 seconds later on a breakaway after a pinpoint pass from St. Louis.

"That was a tough goal," Flyers left wing Simon Gagne said. "'We scored on the first shift, and I think that at that point, we had found what we were trying to build all game. But to give up that third goal, that was a tough break."

"We have two quality teams here," Lightning coach John Tortorella said. "Both teams are trying to get to another spot, and the road isn't big enough for both. Each team is fighting away trying to find their way to four games. "

Darryl Sydor (left), Cory Stillman (center) and Brad Richards (right) celebrate after Stillman scored the first Lightning goal against the Flyers in Game 3. DAN MCDUFFIE/ST. PETERSBURG TIMES

The Lightning's way seemed in a rut after Game 2 at the St. Pete Times Forum with a date against a team that was 6-0 at home.

But the Lightning met before Game 3, and players such as St. Louis, Sydor and captain Dave Andreychuk spoke of the possibility of playing golf by next week. The war of words between Tortorella and Flyers coach Ken Hitchcock also played well.

"We were fired up after all that c— in the newspapers," Boyle said. "It got me fired up. It was kind of like us against everybody else. It was awesome."

Awesome for Tampa Bay was Stillman's goal that opened the scoring with 7:04 left in the first. It was a soft goal as goalie Robert Esche blew what should have been an easy glove save.

Fedotenko's power-play goal came after a neat pass from Andreychuk, and Richards' goal was, as he said, "a no-brainer" after a passing clinic by Boyle, Andre Roy and St. Louis created an open shooting lane from in close.

The defense battled instead of watching as it did in Game 2. And Khabibulin was a wall, or maybe a house. His most important save came when he stopped Primeau from in front of the net 43 seconds after Stillman's goal.

That Khabibulin got help from a crossbar and a post when the Flyers surged in the second period did not diminish the effort.

"The message before the game, without being corny, was seize the moment," Boyle said. "All the things you hear are true. When will you get another chance like this?"

No explanation needed.

SPLITSVILLE—FLYERS EVEN UP SERIES

DAMIAN CRISTODERO

And so it goes in the East final between the Lightning and Flyers. Back and forth. Up and down. Win and lose.

For four consecutive games, the teams alternated levels of play. For four consecutive games, they alternated victories.

It was Philadelphia's turn with a 3-2 win in Game 4 at the Wachovia Center that evened the best-of-seven series at two.

Lightning captain Dave Andreychuk asked, what else did you expect?

"I don't think anyone looked at the matchups and figured one team was going to dominate the other," he said. "No one said it was going to be easy."

After a terrific 4-1 victory in Game 3 and with Game 5 at the St. Pete Times Forum, the top-seeded Lightning had a chance to put a hammerlock on the series.

But the pace the No. 3 Flyers set, especially in the first two periods, was more than the Lightning could handle.

Led by captain Keith Primeau, Philadelphia was physical and made Tampa Bay pay for every inch of ice. The Lightning's lack of physicality hurt, especially on the Flyers' first goal.

"They played a good game, " Lightning center Tim Taylor said. "But I don't feel we came out with the same aggressiveness as Game 3. We have to understand we can't let these games get away."

In a sense, Primeau took it away as Tampa Bay lost for the first time on the road (5-1) and when scoring first (8-1).

His two-on-one short-handed goal, triggered by Andreychuk's turnover, gave the Flyers a 3-1

	1st	2nd	3rd	T
Tampa Bay	1	0	1	**2**
Philadelphia	2	1	0	**3**

lead 11:50 into the second period and was the winner. Primeau also had an assist, won 19 of 28 faceoffs and led Philadelphia's forwards with 22:28 of ice time.

Goalie Robert Esche rebounded from a shaky Game 3 to make 28 saves. John LeClair and Mark Recchi scored 85 seconds apart in the first period for a 2-1 lead, and Philadelphia dominated puck possession and won 39 of 62 faceoffs (63 percent).

Vinny Lecavalier's power-play goal with 32.9 seconds left in the third period, scored six-on-four with goalie Nikolai Khabibulin pulled for an extra skater, was just window dressing.

Primeau's relentless effort drew the most praise.

"Primes has been a guy that we've been looking to and following," LeClair said. "He's really taken charge of a lot of games. And again today, he did the same thing. He was a difference out there every time he went on the ice."

The difference was the final seven minutes of the first period.

Fredrik Modin's power-play goal put the Lightning ahead with 7:13 remaining. But the team wasted the remaining two minutes of Simon Gagne's four-minute high-sticking penalty. And it failed on Esche's slashing penalty that started with nine seconds left on Gagne's. That's 3:51 on the power play, and nothing to show for it.

LeClair tied the score with 3:05 left after Primeau carried the puck to the net, easily avoiding Pavel Kubina's weak stick check and Martin St. Louis, who gave Primeau too much room.

That came after the Lightning did not challenge defenseman Sami Kapanen as he carried the puck through the neutral zone.

"A mental lapse there," Coach John Tortorella said. "We don't play that way. We try to force things in the neutral zone. I felt he was going to be pushed to dump it in, but we gave him the ice."

The Flyers went ahead 2-1 with 1:40 left as Mattias Timander's shot from the high slot deflected off Modin's skate and the shaft of Recchi's stick.

Neither goal was Khabibulin's fault, and the goalie made 23 saves. He said he guessed wrong on Primeau's goal, on which he expected him to pass but Primeau beat him high to the glove side.

"They played a good game, " he said. "We didn't play the game we wanted to play. But you have to give them credit."

"There's no reason to panic," Andreychuk said. "It's 2-2. It's a fun time of year. What else can you ask for?"

Or expect?

Pavel Kubina (13) slams the Flyers' Keith Primeau against the boards during the third period at the Wachovia Center. The Flyers held onto an early lead and tied the series 2-2. DIRK SHADD/ST. PETERSBURG TIMES

ONE STEP CLOSER TO THE CUP

DAMIAN CRISTODERO

It began with Brad Richards telling himself the game against the Flyers was the biggest of his NHL career.

That was not arrogance, the Lightning center said.

	1st	2nd	3rd	T
Philadelphia	0	2	0	**2**
Tampa Bay	1	2	1	**4**

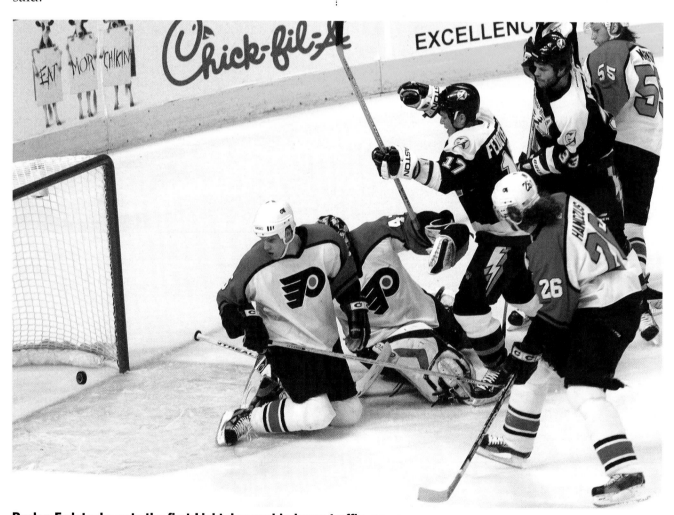

Ruslan Fedotenko nets the first Lightning goal in heavy traffic. BILL SERNE/ST. PETERSBURG TIMES

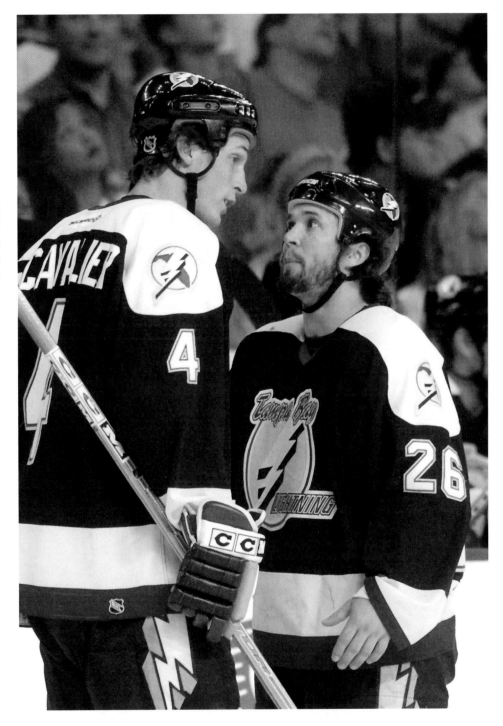

Vincent Lecavalier (left) and Martin St. Louis strategize during the first period of Game 5. Tampa Bay won the game 4-2 to lead the series **3-2.** DIRK SHADD/ST. PETERSBURG TIMES

"But you feel up for the game, " he said. "Not saying that after, but going into it. I said it had to be a big game. "

It turned out to be huge.

Richards scored two goals, including the winner, in Tampa Bay's 4-2 victory over the Flyers in Game 5 of the East final in front of a delirious sell-out crowd of 21,517, the largest ever at the St. Pete Times Forum.

The goals came with a bunch of bells and whistles. Richards' eight goals are a team high, and his five winners lead the playoffs and are one short of the NHL's postseason record.

More important, though, his spark helped the Lightning take a three games to two lead in the best-of-seven series and put it one victory away from a spot in the Stanley Cup Finals.

The first chance to clinch: Thursday in Philadelphia.

"It's a special time of year," Richards said. "Somebody has to step up."

Richards was not alone in a game the players billed as the biggest in the franchise's 12-season history.

Ruslan Fedotenko scored his sixth goal. Nikolai Khabibulin made 28 saves, including 15

during a superb third period in which the Flyers held a 15-6 shot advantage.

Defenseman Pavel Kubina made Keith Primeau his personal project and held the Flyers' captain, who had been such a force in Games 3 and 4, to one shot on goal. And the Lightning power play went 3-for-4.

Not that there weren't some sweaty palms.

After Richards' second goal gave the Lightning a 3-0 lead 7:12 into the second period, the Flyers got two goals in 38 seconds from Michal Handzus and Patrick Sharp to make the score 3-2 at 9:34 and turn a festive atmosphere into one of anxiety.

The crowd let out its collective breath with 15 seconds left on Tim Taylor's empty-net goal.

But Kubina was cautious.

"We still have a long way to go," he said.

Players said the road was made a little shorter during meetings Monday and some reminders before the game. Those were important after the way Tampa Bay was man-handled in a 3-1 loss in Game 4.

"The big key was making the locker room believe we are the better team," defenseman Dan Boyle said.

Said Fedotenko, who gave the Lightning a 1-0 first-period lead: "We reminded each other, and Coach [John Tortorella] reminded us that we needed to play aggressive and we had to continue it the whole game. "

Tampa Bay accomplished everything it wanted in the first period. It outshot the Flyers 18-8 and dictated the physical play. It also killed off a 1:40 four-on-three Flyers power play.

Philadelphia was 0-for-3 on the power play, which made it 1-for-23 for the series.

The Lightning's power play was on target.

Fedotenko scored on a rebound of Boyle's shot. Richards scored 24 seconds into the second period on a slap shot into a top corner of the net on a four-on-three and scored again on a slap shot from the slot after Vinny Lecavalier won a draw and Cory Stillman made a pass.

It was the fifth consecutive power-play goal for the Lightning, whose previous even-strength goal came with 11:40 left in the third period of Game 3.

In that sense, Flyers wing Jeremy Roenick said, "We definitely feel as a team we have owned a better part of the series."

"The difference," Flyers coach Ken Hitchcock said, "is that they won the special teams game and we couldn't finish the point-blank chances we had in the second and third periods."

Philadelphia outshot the Lightning 22-13 in that stretch.

But Khabibulin was outstanding and in a memorable 15-second stretch early in the third period made terrific stops on Roenick and Mark Recchi.

The Tampa Bay bench congratulates Brad Richards after he scored his second-period power-play goal. DIRK SHADD/ST. PETERSBURG TIMES

IT'S NOT OVER YET

DAMIAN CRISTODERO

Dan Boyle, sitting alone and still in his sweaty T-shirt and shorts, replayed Game 6 of the East final over and over in his mind. Every time, he shook his head.

Finally, for emphasis, it seemed, the Lightning defenseman let out a long sigh.

"I just don't know what to say," Boyle said. "It was tough."

And it is about to get tougher.

The Flyers' 5-4 overtime victory, in front of a roof-raising crowd of 19,910 at the Wachovia Center, tied the series at three games apiece and set up a deciding Game 7 at the St. Pete Times Forum.

That Tampa Bay lost, and lost its first chance to clinch a spot in the Stanley Cup Finals, was bad enough. That it was less than two minutes away from winning prompted the stunned reactions in the locker room.

Simon Gagne's second goal with 1:42 left in the extra period was the winner. But it would not have happened without an extraordinary effort by Flyers captain Keith Primeau on the tying goal with 1:49 left in the third period.

"That," Boyle said, "was one of the toughest goals I've ever been associated with if not the toughest. We'd better regroup real quick."

And store for future reference how the game turned, in part, because the Lightning, with a 4-3 lead entering the third period, lost their forecheck and stopped forcing the play. Instead, they played not to lose and were outshot 27-10 in the third period and overtime and 43-29 overall.

Despite all that, Tampa Bay, paced by two goals each from Vinny Lecavalier and Ruslan Fedotenko, two assists each from Martin St. Louis and Dave Andreychuk, and 38 saves by Nikolai Khabibulin, had a chance.

"But we collapsed," Boyle said.

	1st	2nd	3rd	OT	T
Tampa Bay	1	3	0	0	4
Philadelphia	2	1	1	1	5

And the Flyers surged.

"Desperate teams are dangerous because you throw everything but the kitchen sink at them," Primeau said. "That's why Game 7s are so exciting to watch because both teams are desperate."

Primeau was the most desperate. With two goals and two assists, and with grinding physical play, he set an example and the tone.

He scored the tying goal after gathering a rebound, kicking the puck through the crease and circling the Lightning net before putting it past Khabibulin. He also assisted on the winner in which Gagne fired from in close through Khabibulin's legs.

But the Flyers also got help from Tampa Bay.

Mistakes by Pavel Kubina, Darryl Sydor and Brad Lukowich led to Philadelphia's first three goals. Sydor's was especially egregious as his blind backhand pass into the slot went to the point to Vladimir Malakhov, who passed to Primeau for an easy goal that gave the Flyers a 2-1 first-period lead.

"I tried to make a play," Sydor said. "I [bleeped] up."

Lecavalier's goal 45 seconds into the second period tied the score. Sami Kapanen's goal with 7:18 left, on a shot from a faceoff circle that Khabibulin should have stopped, made the score 3-2.

Fedotenko's two goals, both from the slot off passes from Andreychuk, with 4:45 and 2:27 left in the second put Tampa Bay in front but also set up the disappointing finish.

That it didn't come sooner is testament to Khabibulin, who was brilliant in the third period, when Tampa Bay was outshot 17-5.

"Our game is very aggressive," Boyle said. "At times, we were very passive. The times we were aggressive, we made bad plays. The way we were playing, it was just a matter of time."

"It's disappointing," Lecavalier said. "We were so close. We should have kept coming at them offensively."

Center Tim Taylor listened to the painful analysis. He finally said, "Enough."

"It doesn't do us any good to go over it; none whatsoever," he said. " Game 7 is coming up in a day and a half. Moping around does us no good."

"The stage is set," Boyle said. "It's up to us to show how we can regroup. The most important thing is to realize we may never get this opportunity again, so we have to give it all we've got."

Vincent Lecavalier (left) takes a fist to the face from Flyer Kim Johnsson during the overtime period. The Flyers won in overtime thanks to a goal by Simon Gagne. DIRK SHADD/ST. PETERSBURG TIMES

BELIEVE IT!
LIGHTNING MAKE FINALS

DAMIAN CRISTODERO

Every now and then, you figure you've seen just about everything.

Think of how you shook your head when Tampa Bay went four consecutive seasons, from 1997-98 to 2000-01, with at least 50 losses. Think of

	1st	2nd	3rd	T
Philadelphia	0	1	0	**1**
Tampa Bay	1	1	0	**2**

The Lightning celebrate on the ice after Fredrik Modin's goal in the second period put Tampa Bay ahead of the Flyers. The score held up and sent the Lightning to the Stanley Cup Finals.
DIRK SHADD/ST. PETERSBURG TIMES

Flyers center Keith Primeau crashes into the goal while trying to score in the second period. Nikolai Khabibulin makes the save in front of Pavel Kubina. DIRK SHADD/ST. PETERSBURG TIMES

how you looked away during 1997-98 when the team had two 16-game winless streaks.

Now think of this: With their 2-1 victory over the Flyers in Game 7 of the East final, in front of a crowd of 22,117, the largest ever at the St. Pete Times Forum, the Lightning, yes *the Lightning*, are going to face the Flames for the Stanley Cup. Game 1 is this Tuesday at the St. Pete Times Forum.

"This," center Tim Taylor said, "is the best feeling I've had in a long time."

Not only because Tampa Bay won the series and its first conference title four games to three. But because of the circumstances that were supposed to expose the Lightning as an inexperienced, shaky playoff newcomer.

The Lightning were irreparably damaged, many assumed, after a distressing overtime loss in Game 6 in which it led with less than two minutes remaining. But the team regrouped and, in the process, showed the resiliency that marked much of its season.

The team also made sure the 2-1 lead it had entering the third period was secure and outshot the Flyers 8-7. This was after a third period in Game 6 in which it was on its heels, outshot 15-6 and saw its one-goal lead disappear with 1:49 left.

"For them to answer, it was a mental toughness," Lightning coach John Tortorella said. "It was something our guys handled very well. Our team has matured. For them to win the game is a great sign for this hockey club."

"It shows that we were together," center Vinny Lecavalier said. "It could have been a game we lost. We started out a little flat-footed, but then we went after them."

Ruslan Fedotenko scored his ninth goal on the power play in the first period. Fredrik Modin scored his seventh in the second for a 2-0 lead. Brad Richards had two assists, and Nikolai Khabibulin made 22 saves, including one on Keith Primeau's breakaway with 6:56 left in the second period that preserved the one-goal lead.

The only blip was Kim Johnsson's goal with 9:44 remaining in the second that got past Khabibulin after deflecting in front off the stick of Lightning defenseman Nolan Pratt.

"The disappointment is immense," Flyers wing Jeremy Roenick said. "It's to the point you feel like you're going to throw up. You are sick to your stomach."

"It's all empty," Johnsson said. "It's the worst feeling in the world. It's like you can't feel anything."

The Lightning were feeling it, again, on the power play.

Fedotenko's goal with 3:14 left in the first period—a double deflection off his shaft after Martin St. Louis tipped Richards' point shot—was Tampa Bay's ninth power-play goal of the series and fifth in its previous six chances. It also helped calm Tampa Bay, as did two previous penalty kills that left Philadelphia 1-for-26 in the series with the extra man.

"They came at us pretty hard, and the two penalty kills, I think, were the turning point," Richards said. "Then we get a power play and scored right away. It really took the nerves out and got us going."

Modin made a huge play along the boards to knock the puck out of the zone when the Flyers were pushing in the final minute.

And then there was captain Dave Andreychuk, who at 40 and in his 22nd season finally made it to a Cup finals.

"You dream about this day happening," he said. "You don't know how you're going to feel. I don't really feel relief. I feel excitement more than anything else. Everybody in our locker room should be pretty proud of the situation we're in."

"We're very happy where we are," defenseman Brad Lukowich said. "It's a great accomplishment, but we're not content."

But they are light years away from the team that won just once in a 29-game stretch in 1999-2000, and the one that won just twice in a 25-game stretch in 2000-01.

"This answers the question that the Tampa Bay Lightning can play through a grind," Tortorella said.

Maybe we haven't seen anything yet.

Following Tampa Bay's win over Philadelphia, Bill Daly, NHL executive VP and chief legal officer, presents the Prince of Wales Trophy to Lightning captain Dave Andreychuk. DIRK SHADD/ST. PETERSBURG TIMES

#25 DAVE ANDREYCHUK

At some point before the Lightning face the Flames in Game 1 of the Stanley Cup Finals, Dave Andreychuk will take a walk.

The Lightning captain does this every game day. It clears his mind, loosens his legs and helps him focus on the task at hand. Andreychuk said he has walked since his second NHL season in Buffalo when assistant coach Red Berenson advised him.

"He said it made him feel good, so I've been doing it ever since," Andreychuk said.

Berenson, though, likely never walked on air, which is what Andreychuk has done the past few days. The left wing, 40, in his 22nd season and a sure Hall of Famer as one of the NHL's great goal scorers, is playing in his first Stanley Cup Finals.

Fulfilling that dream has been the main reason Andreychuk has not retired. It is why he increased his summer conditioning program. And it was a catalyst in his transformation from a pure goal scorer into a valuable checking forward and faceoff specialist.

But Andreychuk said it is not about winning a championship to secure his place in league history and his career will be just fine without one. It is simply about taking the next and most dramatic step in a career that has been as much about evolution as contributions.

How big will it be when Andreychuk skates onto the ice? Consider he admitted to a silent yelp of delight when it sank in he finally would play for the Cup.

And consider that as the seconds counted down in the Lightning's Game 7 victory over the Flyers, Andreychuk's parents, Julian and Roz, wife Sue and sister Sandra were in the stands, arms locked and crying.

Height: 6'4"
Weight: 220
Position: LW
Shoots: Right
Born: September 29, 1963
Hamilton, Ontario

"For them it was a great day," Andreychuk said. "The emotions have been building up for quite some time. I feel good, not only for me but for them. They've been behind me the whole time."

The ultimate credit, though, is Andreychuk's, and it goes well beyond his 634 goals, 11th all-time; his NHL-high 270 power-play goals; and his 19 20-goal seasons, behind only Gordie Howe (22) and Ron Francis (20).

Andreychuk has reinvented himself in the latter stages of his career. Once known only for scoring prowess, he has morphed into a doggedly determined checker, penalty killer and faceoff man.

He can still score. His soft hands and nose for the net helped him to 21 goals and a third consecutive 20-goal season for Tampa Bay. But the other elements in his game—his determination on the puck, his long reach that gets his stick into passing lanes, taking defensive-zone faceoffs—have ensured Andreychuk a place in a game ruled by the speed and skill of the young.

"He's just one of those guys you want to win the Cup for," Dan Boyle said. "It's not like he's a fourth-line guy chipping in seven or eight minutes a game. He's one of our big guys."

And Andreychuk wants it badly. His 1,597 regular-season games are seventh all-time and the most of any player without a Cup. But he knows so many variables go into winning, it is foolish to count on it.

Said Tortorella: "I think Dave would prefer right now that it wasn't about him getting in [the final]. It's about the Tampa Bay Lightning getting in. That's what he brings to the team, the understanding that it's not really an individual-type thing. We are here together. Dave doesn't need to be legitimized anymore. He's a Hall of Famer."

Julian said that is not his son's motivation.

"It's been a tremendous ride on the roller coaster of the hockey world," Julian said. "Not riding the highest roller coaster does not mean you didn't have a great time as you go along.

"So many don't make it this far. For him, he's had a tremendous ride."

Not to mention those nice little walks. —DAMIAN CRISTODERO

Veteran Dave Andreychuk hoists the Stanley Cup after he helped the Lightning defeat the Calgary Flames in the Finals. DAN MCDUFFIE/ST. PETERSBURG TIMES

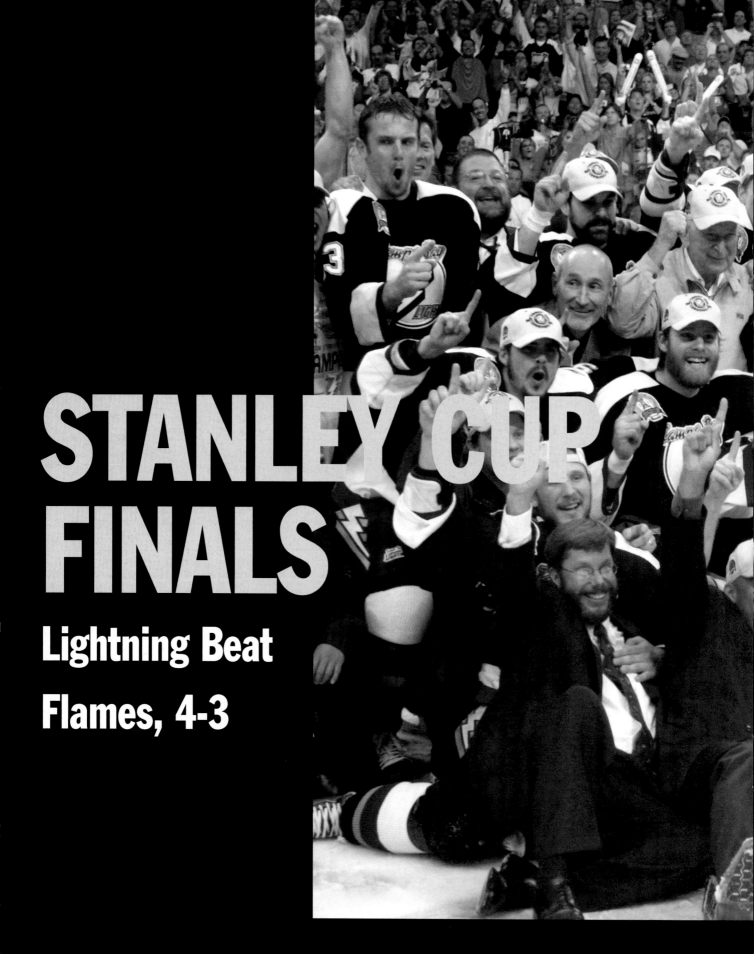

STANLEY CUP FINALS

Lightning Beat Flames, 4-3

FLAMEOUT—CALGARY TAKES GAME 1

DAMIAN CRISTODERO

Disappointing not demoralizing. Unfortunate not catastrophic. Those were the sentiments kickin' around the Lightning locker room after their 4-1 loss to the Flames in Game 1 of the Stanley Cup Finals.

	1st	2nd	3rd	T
Calgary	1	2	1	**4**
Tampa Bay	0	0	1	**1**

Calgary's Chris Simon gets a shot by Lightning goaltender Nikolai Khabibulin for the fourth and final goal. The Flames took the first game of the finals, 4-1. DIRK SHADD/ST. PETERSBURG TIMES

Calgary's Robyn Regehr (28) checks Martin St. Louis into the boards. DAN MCDUFFIE/ST. PETERSBURG TIMES

Even left wing Dave Andreychuk answered questions with good humor. But that all ended when the talk turned to Game 2.

Asked if it is too early in a seven-game series to call it a must-win, Andreychuk said, "No."

The captain let that sink in for a moment before continuing.

"It is a must-win for us," he said. "We don't want to go down oh-and-two. It's not the end of the world, but you probably could see it."

It will be interesting to see how Tampa Bay responds. The team is behind in a series for the first time this postseason, and the players appeared baffled as to why they didn't come out with more hop, especially considering the thunderous blastoff provided by the crowd of 21,674, the second largest ever at the St. Pete Times Forum.

"We just didn't come out as hard as we needed to," defenseman Dan Boyle said. "I can't tell you why."

Jitters? Maybe. A letdown from a physical, emotional East final with the Flyers? Perhaps.

Whatever the cause, Andreychuk said, "Our desperation has to get back to where it was last series. This team is not looking for a split. They are looking to win both these games and go back to Calgary 2-0."

Martin St. Louis scored on the power play 4:13 into the third period. It was his first goal in six games, but that only made the score 3-1. And whatever momentum Tampa Bay garnered was dampened by three subsequent penalties.

But there were more pressing concerns.

A disappointed Vincent Lecavalier skates off the ice as the Flames celebrate their third goal. DIRK SHADD/ST. PETERSBURG TIMES

Tampa Bay struggled with its passing for most of the night. Instead of turning to a simpler game, it tried to force its way through Calgary's aggressive forecheck.

Calgary also won the races to the loose pucks and many of the one-on-one battles. The result

was Miikka Kiprusoff needed only to be solid while making 23 saves.

With 19 shots, it wasn't as if the Flames were overwhelming. But they took advantage of their chances. They also got some bounces. Some were caused by very choppy ice. But as St. Louis said, "Yeah, they got good bounces, but they worked for their bounces."

Bounces that resulted in Martin Gelinas' goal 3:02 into the game. Andrew Ference's shot from the high slot hit Andreychuk, Flames center Craig Conroy, Gelinas, the post and the skate of goalie Nikolai Khabibulin before sliding into the net.

Another bounce sent what seemed to be a perfect pass from Andreychuk over Fredrik Modin's stick. It turned into a short-handed breakaway for Jarome Iginla and a 2-0 Calgary lead with 4:39 left in the second period. Stephane Yelle's goal with 1:52 left after Boyle's turnover in the Lightning zone made it 3-0. But it was Iginla's goal, his playoff-high 11th, that was the back-breaker.

It also highlighted a superb effort by Calgary's penalty killers. Tampa Bay, which scored nine power-play goals against the Flyers, was 1-for-5.

"They were aggressive," Modin said. "I felt we didn't have a chance to get up with our power play. We didn't get too much out of it."

"We're trying to skate and trying to create chances and put some pressure on them," Iginla said. "It also was a good break, too."

After Khabibulin stopped Iginla, the puck bounced to Khabibulin's right. Modin, trailing the play, went around the net to Khabibulin's left. That gave Iginla a chance to retrieve the puck and shoot again at the fallen goaltender.

"I didn't see where it was," Modin said. "I just went to the other side."

In Game 2, Tampa Bay must find another level. But a must-win?

"I think all games are must-wins," Lightning coach John Tortorella said. "If you don't approach it that way, I think you're approaching it wrong."

For the Lightning, that would be catastrophic.

LIGHTNING REIGNITED!

DAMIAN CRISTODERO

The Lightning locker room was quiet before Game 2 of the Stanley Cup Finals. There was no rock music blaring. No one felt the need to make a dramatic speech.

It was just the way defenseman Nolan Pratt likes it.

"When we're quiet before games, it seems like we're really ready," he said. "Very focused."

The noise came later.

The Lightning's 4-1 victory over the Flames in front of a crowd of 22,222, the largest ever at the St. Pete Times Forum, evened the best-of-seven series at one game apiece and helped erase the memory of a terrible loss in Game 1.

But it also seemed to signal the end of this quaint little series between two low-payroll, hard-working teams.

There were 32 penalties for 124 minutes. Twenty-four, a record for a period in a final, for 108 came in the third, with four fighting majors, game

	1st	2nd	3rd	T
Calgary	0	0	1	**1**
Tampa Bay	1	0	3	**4**

Tampa Bay's Nolan Pratt punches Shean Donovan in front of the goal early in the game. DIRK SHADD/ST. PETERSBURG TIMES

misconducts to Calgary's Martin Gelinas and Tampa Bay's Chris Dingman, and 10-minute misconducts to Flames Chris Simon and Chuck Kobasew, and Dingman and Pavel Kubina of Tampa Bay.

The game ended with Lightning enforcer Andre Roy threatening Andrew Ference, who ear-lier fought Cory Stillman in what seemed to be an attempt at payback for an elbow Stillman threw at Marcus Nilson in Game 1.

"Nobody likes to lose," Lightning wing Ruslan Fedotenko said. "They tried to send a message. It was a great job by our guys when we responded."

Ruslan Fedotenko follows the rebound of his first shot and beats Calgary goaltender Miikka Kiprusoff (34) for the Lightning's first goal. Tampa Bay won the game 4-1 and tied the series. DIRK SHADD/ST. PETERSBURG TIMES

"It's not like we have a lot of hate for this team," wing Martin St. Louis said. "But you have to have some hate for your opponent. That makes you able to beat them in the playoffs."

The rough stuff was just an exclamation point on the Lightning's fine effort.

Fedotenko's 10th goal of the playoffs put Tampa Bay ahead 7:10 into the first. The Lightning broke it open with goals from Brad Richards, Dan Boyle and Martin St. Louis in a span of 3:07 of the third to make it 4-0 at 5:58.

Richards' goal was his ninth of the postseason and sixth winner, which tied the mark of Colorado's Joe Sakic (1996) and Dallas' Joe Nieuwendyk (1999).

Richards also had an assist. Captain Dave Andreychuk had two as did Vinny Lecavalier, who was physical and played his best overall game of the playoffs. Goalie Nikolai Khabibulin rebounded from a so-so effort in Game 1 to make 18 saves.

Ville Nieminen got Calgary's goal on the power play with 7:39 left in the third.

"They outscored us and outplayed us," Flames defenseman Dave Lowry said. "That's two pretty important things. We let them take it to us. We were on our heels and they took all the momentum."

"We knew," Lightning coach John Tortorella said. "We knew we were going to play the game we were supposed to play the first game but didn't. It's a mindset."

A mindset that got straightened out during a long and brutal video session.

"I'm not so sure I was calm between games," Tortorella said. "We were honest. You need to evaluate yourself, understand where you are as a club, and look for answers and try to find a response."

Tampa Bay responded in the first period by killing off four Flames power plays and 6 of 7 in the game. They won 67 percent of faceoffs including a 12-for-16 effort from Lecavalier and a 10-for-14 effort from Richards.

The Lightning outshot Calgary 31-19, including 13-4 in the third, and blocked numerous shots with bodies and sticks.

The aesthetics were pleasing too. Lecavalier's pass to himself off the back of the Flames' net helped set up Fedotenko's goal. And Andreychuk's effort to dig the puck away from Calgary's Stephane Yelle in the slot led to Richards'.

The power play was just 1-for-9 with St. Louis scoring on a five-on-three. But the team played with the determination and intensity so lacking in Game 1.

"It makes a huge difference if guys have their legs going," Pratt said. "We got off to the start we wanted and created the momentum."

Nothing quiet about that.

Dan Boyle (22) receives congratulations from his teammates after scoring in the third period. DIRK SHADD/ST. PETERSBURG TIMES

LIGHTNING'S HOPES CRUSHED AFTER LOSS

DAMIAN CRISTODERO

The question was never asked, but Dan Boyle decided to answer it nonetheless.

The Lightning defenseman said no one in the locker room is talking about throwing in the towel. The confidence is still there, as is the resolve.

	1st	2nd	3rd	T
Tampa Bay	0	0	0	**0**
Calgary	0	2	1	**3**

Tampa Bay's Andre Roy (36) and Nikolai Khabibulin battle in the net against Calgary's Martin Gelinas. Calgary scored three goals and shut out the Lightning in Game 3. DIRK SHADD/ST. PETERSBURG TIMES

Ruslan Fedotenko takes a hard hit into the board from the Flames' Robyn Regehr. The hit resulted in an injury and Fedotenko was taken to the hospital. DIRK SHADD/ST. PETERSBURG TIMES

"There is no quit in this team," Boyle said. "We're not going to give up by any means."

The sentiment might seem extreme considering Tampa Bay trails in the best-of-seven Stanley Cup Finals just two games to one. But that is how hard the players took the 3-0 loss to the Flames at the Pengrowth Saddledome.

The Lightning failed to build on the momentum they created in their Game 2 victory. They let Calgary take away the initiative for a stretch in the second period that cost two goals, and they failed to capitalize on some significant chances.

Not that there were that many. Tampa Bay took just 11 shots in the first two periods, but Fredrik Modin and Brad Richards could not convert on prime opportunities that would have broken a 0-0 second-period tie.

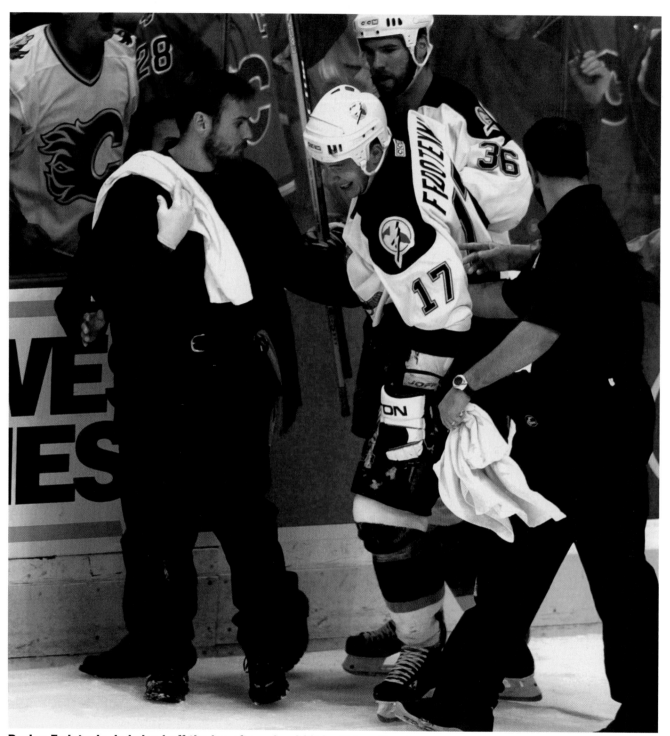

Ruslan Fedotenko is helped off the ice after a hard hit by Robyn Regehr. DIRK SHADD/ST. PETERSBURG TIMES

"You can't expect to win with just 10 shots in two periods," Richards said.

Still, "We had chances," Boyle said. "I'm sure a few guys in this room will be kicking themselves. When you get chances, you have to bury them."

More trouble: the Lightning will hear more about wing Ruslan Fedotenko's. The team leader with 10 playoff goals was taken to the hospital after he was pushed into the top of the boards face-first by Flames defenseman Robyn Regehr with 5:47 left in the third period and sustained a deep cut and ugly bruise on his right cheek.

For the Flames and their red-clad fans in the sellout crowd of 19,221, things could not have been better.

Chris Simon and Shean Donovan scored in 3:16 of the second period to give Calgary a 2-0 lead with 2:51 left. And goalie Miikka Kiprusoff had 21 saves for his playoff-high fifth shutout.

Then there was Jarome Iginla. The captain scored the Flames' last goal late in the third period (the team's second on the power play), assisted on Simon's and fought Vinny Lecavalier in a battle that was the highlight of a hard-hitting first period in which both teams tried to establish their turf.

"The fight is just part of the intensity out there," Iginla said. "Everybody knows what is on the line. Both teams really raised their game physically last game and I thought we really upped it as a group. The fight just happened."

Neither player inflicted any damage. The Lightning failed to do so as well.

Modin had the puck alone in front of Kiprusoff but fired high and wide 3:30 into the second period. Richards thought he had the goalie beaten on a short-handed breakaway, but the wrist shot hit the shaft of Kiprusoff's stick with 6:23 remaining.

Sixteen seconds later, Simon scored a power-play goal when his third shot beat goalie Nikolai Khabibulin after two were valiantly blocked by a sprawled Modin.

Donovan scored on a two-on-one after he picked off Lecavalier's pass from behind the Flames' net that was intended for Modin, but it went behind him and went to the Flames' wing.

Lightning coach John Tortorella said he believed Simon's goal was the turning point. Defenseman Brad Lukowich created the short-handed situation by turning the puck over, then taking a slashing penalty. Defenseman Darryl Sydor fell at the Flames blue line and partner Pavel Kubina was out of position in a corner.

But Richards saw it differently.

"I had it in my head they were going to score," he said. "If I had scored on that, things might have been different."

Things might have been different had the Lightning converted one of their four power plays and not sagged after Simon's goal while the Flames surged.

"We let them take control of the game after the first goal," captain Dave Andreychuk said. "It's just a goal. It's one shot."

"We just need a better team effort," Boyle said. "Everybody is working hard."

No one, he reiterated, is giving up.

JUST IN THE NIK OF TIME

DAMIAN CRISTODERO

Center Brad Richards admitted the Lightning will get zero style points for the way they played Game 4 of the Stanley Cup Finals.

"Very ugly," he said at one point.

"It wasn't pretty," he said at another.

	1st	2nd	3rd	T
Tampa Bay	1	0	0	**1**
Calgary	0	0	0	**0**

Ice flies as the Lightning's Cory Stillman and the Flames' Robyn Regehr chase the puck. DAN MCDUFFIE/ST. PETERSBURG TIMES

Goaltender Nikolai Khabibulin and Vincent Lecavalier, Jassen Cullimore and Darryl Sydor defend the goal against Calgary's Martin Gelinas. The Flames were held scoreless in the game. DIRK SHADD/ST. PETERSBURG TIMES

But you know what? Tampa Bay will take its 1-0 victory over the Flames at the Pengrowth Saddledome and cherish it as if it were its most perfectly played game.

The bottom line is the same.

The win not only tied the best-of-seven series at two games apiece, Tampa Bay reclaimed home-ice advantage as two of the final three games are at the St. Pete Times Forum.

Richards scored his 10th playoff goal and his NHL-record seventh winner with a five-on-three power-play goal 2:48 into the game. Nikolai Khabibulin improved to 6-0 in games after a loss and made 29 saves for his fifth shutout of the post-season.

And Tampa Bay got a huge break when it played the final 4:11 on a power play after Ville Nieminen received a five-minute major for elbowing Vinny Lecavalier's head into the side glass.

Lecavalier did not speak to reporters after the game, and Coach John Tortorella declined to address it other than to say Lecavalier "will be fine." But defenseman Cory Sarich said, "Emotions run high. I'm not going to say whether it was dirty or clean, but we'll take it, thank you very much."

Give the Lightning credit for holding up under exasperating circumstances.

Already without 10-goal scorer Ruslan Fedotenko (lacerated right cheek), Tampa Bay also played without defenseman Pavel Kubina because of an undisclosed lower-body injury.

That forced right wing Ben Clymer and center Martin Cibak to play their first Stanley Cup Finals games. Both performed well. Clymer got 8:12 of ice time while Cibak got 7:16 and had two shots on goal.

"The focus tonight was making sure we were competing for the full 60 minutes," Sarich said. "We just wanted to spend as much time in their end as we could. Really takes the pressure off us as defensemen."

Richards did his part with his slap shot off a feed from Dave Andreychuk. The Lightning are 8-0 in the playoffs when Richards scores and 30-0-2 all season.

"I'd rather not talk about the game winners anymore," said Richards, who broke the record of Colorado's Joe Sakic (1996) and Dallas' Joe Nieuwendyk (1999). "We won the game. It was a big goal for momentum."

The talk, though, was whether a five-on-three was warranted as referee Kerry Fraser called Mike Commodore for holding Fredrik Modin and Chris Clark for cross-checking Nolan Pratt.

"What is a penalty in the second shift is not a penalty in the first shift," Flames coach Darryl Sutter said. "A penalty in the second shift, not a penalty in the third period. Whatever. It was a hell of a hockey game."

The Flames pressed throughout the game. And Calgary dominated territorially. There were times it kept the puck in the offensive zone for extended periods.

But Tampa Bay battled as hard as it has all series, especially below the defensive hash marks. Calgary had 29 shots and outshot the Lightning 12-5 in the third. But many shots came from the outside, where Khabibulin had a good look.

"It was a great team effort," Khabibulin said. "It's always nice to get that first goal early in the game. But no matter what happens, I have to stay focused."

"I thought Nik was outstanding," Tortorella said. "To compete and stay within it here, your goaltender has to be your best player. I thought this was Nik's best game of this round."

Tampa Bay needs to do it again in Game 5. The team has

not won consecutive games since Games 3 and 4 of the East semifinals.

Richards said it will take "urgency, desperation" and "a work ethic in which we block everything else out."

No need for it to be pretty. As Tortorella said about Game 4, "I thought it was really ugly at times. We score one. They don't score any. So we win. That's the way it goes."

Nikolai Khabibulin works hard to make a stick save in the third period of the shutout. DIRK SHADD/ST. PETERSBURG TIMES

OT LOSS EXTRA PAINFUL

DAMIAN CRISTODERO

Lightning center Tim Taylor sat in front of his locker, more frustrated than exhausted, more upset than disappointed.

Tampa Bay had just lost Game 5 of the Stanley Cup Finals 3-2 in overtime to the Flames. As if that

	1st	2nd	3rd	OT	T
Calgary	1	1	0	1	**3**
Tampa Bay	1	0	1	0	**2**

The Flames pile into the goal, but they are unable to stop a shot by Martin St. Louis in the first period. DIRK SHADD/ST. PETERSBURG TIMES

Nikolai Khabibulin makes a save in the first period, but it was not enough as Tampa Bay eventually lost the game in overtime, 3-2. BILL SERNE/ST. PETERSBURG TIMES

wasn't bad enough, the Lightning center said it was as much his team's doing as Calgary's.

"We didn't respond well," Taylor said. "It feels like your heart is ripped out right now."

The final piece was torn away by Flames left wing Oleg Saprykin, whose rebound shot got past goalie Nikolai Khabibulin with 5:20 left in the extra period and silenced a crowd of 22,426, the largest ever at the St. Pete Times Forum.

With a three games to two lead in the best-of-seven series, the Flames have two chances to win their first Cup since 1989. The first: Saturday in Calgary.

"It's just a great feeling, a great feeling for every guy in the room," Saprykin said. "Guys battled hard, and every guy deserved it. It doesn't matter who scored the goal. We just tried to stay for each other."

Jarome Iginla scored his playoff-high 13th goal and had an assist. And goalie Miikka Kiprusoff improved to 4-0 in Game 5s this postseason with 26 saves.

On the other hand...

"Our mindset needs to be different," Lightning left wing Chris Dingman said.

"They came after us and played hard, but we didn't do the things we talked about, the things we needed to do."

Such as churning the legs at all times, winning the battles along the boards and limiting turnovers and mistakes. And what the heck happened in the second period, when the Lightning played one of their worst periods of the playoffs and were outshot 14-3?

Make no mistake, the Flames deserved to win this game. They were quicker to the puck and hungrier to retrieve it.

"We know we have to play a lot better," Lightning captain Dave Andreychuk said. "They took the play to us. We turned the puck over more than we did the game before and didn't get the puck deep."

Vinny Lecavalier's turnover at the Flames' blue line and a badly timed and executed line change gave Calgary an odd-man situation in its offensive zone and led to Saprykin's goal off a rebound of Iginla's shot.

It was Martin St. Louis' errant pass in the offensive zone that led to Iginla's goal that gave Calgary a 2-1 lead with 4:50 left in the second. And it was Fredrik Modin's high stick in the offensive zone that gave the Flames a power play on which Martin Gelinas scored on a great tip-in to give Calgary a 1-0 lead 2:13 into the game.

Still, the Lightning teased their fans. St. Louis' goal with 33.5 seconds left in the first period tied the score at one. And Modin's power-play goal 37 seconds into the third period tied it at two.

But as Coach John Tortorella said, "You're not going to win Game 5 in the finals playing 40 minutes like we played tonight. It simply comes back and bites you in the [butt]."

Not everything was negative. Khabibulin made 33 saves, some brilliant, including an astonishing right-leg stop of Iginla in the first period to preserve the one-goal deficit.

Sure, he would like to have Iginla's goal back.

Martin St. Louis falls to the ice on top of Calgary's Chris Clark. DIRK SHADD/ST. PETERSBURG TIMES

Maybe he was guarding the short side too much. But the shot to the long side was professional, low and hard.

And the line of center Martin Cibak and wings Dingman and Ben Clymer was Tampa Bay's best. No offense, but that can't happen.

"We have to play better in front of Nik," Taylor said. "It's about time we gave him a great game. Game 2 is the only game I think we came to play with a lot of heart and desperation."

That will not cut it in Game 6.

"We have to get angry," Taylor said. "We all have these dreams and aspirations of winning this thing.

"We have to get angry and ticked off because they are taking it away from us."

That's not disappointment. That's anger.

ONE LAST SHOT

DAMIAN CRISTODERO

As far as the Lightning were concerned, Game 6 of the Stanley Cup Finals might as well have been Game 7.

Lose and the season was over.

"We're thinking of it as Game 7," center Vinny Lecavalier said before the game. "If all goes well, we'll deal with the next game after that. We're confident. We believe in ourselves, and that's all you need."

	1st	2nd	3rd	OT	OT2	T
Tampa Bay	0	2	0	0	1	**3**
Calgary	0	2	0	0	0	**2**

What Tampa Bay got was a dramatic 3-2 double-overtime victory over the Flames at the Pengrowth Saddledome to tie the best-of-seven

Martin St. Louis scores the game-winning goal against Flames goalie Miikka Kiprusoff during the second overtime period. The Lightning tied the series, 3-3, with the win. DAN MCDUFFIE/ST. PETERSBURG TIMES

Martin Gelinas (23) takes a shot in the third period, but goaltender Nikolai Khabibulin makes the save in spite of Flame Oleg Saprykin falling over his back. DIRK SHADD/ST. PETERSBURG TIMES

series at three games apiece and force the real Game 7 at the St. Pete Times Forum.

"We have a chance of a lifetime," Lightning center Tim Taylor said.

Martin St. Louis got the winner 33 seconds into the second overtime after Calgary goalie Miikka Kiprusoff stopped Taylor's shot from the point.

"I was just trying to put it on net," St. Louis said. "At that point in time, it's not the pretty goal that's going to win. I was waiting to see if the rebound would come. It wasn't a good angle, but I just threw it on net. You never know."

"It's awesome," Lightning defenseman Dan Boyle said. "We celebrated for about 30 seconds, and then we realized we [only] won Game 6."

Brad Richards scored twice on the power play in the second and has a team-high 12 goals in the postseason.

But Calgary matched with goals by Chris Clark and Marcus Nilson, who tied the score at two with 2:11 remaining in the period.

It was the first time the teams were tied entering the third period. And that period sparked what could have been a huge controversy.

It occurred with about seven minutes remaining in the third period on what appeared to be a Calgary goal but was, according to the league, without definitive proof.

Calgary's Oleg Saprykin centered the puck from the left of the Lightning net. It hit the stick of goalie Nikolai Khabibulin and ended up in front. Martin Gelinas slid toward the crease and nudged the puck forward with his right skate.

A replay appeared to show the puck against Khabibulin's right pad and over the goal line just before he kicked it out. The goal light never went on, and no signal was made by the referees.

Martin St. Louis displays his game face in Game 6 of the Stanley Cup Finals. DIRK SHADD/ST. PETERSBURG TIMES

The play was reviewed by the NHL from multiple angles and no definitive ruling could be made. Calgary coach Darryl Sutter said he did not believe it was a goal.

Had it been determined the puck was over the goal line, the next question would have been if Gelinas had kicked it.

The Flames almost scored about three minutes into the game as Craig Conroy tried to go around the Lightning net on a wraparound. Khabibulin was slow going from right post to left. But Darryl Sydor was in position to get his stick on the puck.

Dave Andreychuk had a fine opportunity at 8:12, when he stole the puck from Calgary defenseman Toni Lydman to Kiprusoff's left. Andreychuk spun to gain separation from Lydman, but Kiprusoff saved the backhander.

The Flames outshot Tampa Bay 13-5 in the second period but ended tied at two. The Lightning made the most of their first power play by taking a 1-0 lead 4:17 into the period.

Richards, to Kiprusoff's left, was trying to pass cross-slot to Andreychuk. But Kiprusoff pushed his glove out to deflect the puck. He did—but into the net.

The Flames got it back on a tremendous play by Ville Nieminen and questionable defense from Tampa Bay's Cory Stillman.

Clark scored on an easy tap-in at 9:05. But Nieminen's spinaround pass was perfectly placed between Stillman, who seemed late on the back check, and defenseman Dan Boyle.

The Lightning went ahead on Richards' second power-play goal of the game with 9:08 left in the period. It was all Richards. After the puck came out of a scrum along the right wing boards, the center stole it off the stick of Nilson and fired low past Kiprusoff.

Nilson made amends when he tied the score at two with 2:11 left.

The sequence began when Boyle tried to bat down a floating puck in the Lightning zone. He did but right to Saprykin.

Boyle, off balance, also twisted away from Saprykin, who sprinted forward.

When Nolan Pratt went to cover Saprykin, he left Nilson alone. Saprykin's pass was perfect.

Flames goalie Miikka Kiprusoff skates slowly off the ice as Lightning team members celebrate their Game 6 double-overtime win. DAN MCDUFFIE/ST. PETERSBURG TIMES

LORDS OF THE RINK

DAMIAN CRISTODERO

Oh... my... God.

What other reaction can you have, really? You've seen the Lightning lose 50 games four years in a row; including overtime, of course, but why quibble?

You've seen 16-game winless streaks twice in the same season. And just two years ago, Tampa Bay didn't make the playoffs.

	1st	2nd	3rd	T
Calgary	0	0	1	**1**
Tampa Bay	1	1	0	**2**

But rub your eyes, shake the cobwebs out of your head and get a load of this.

A shot by Ruslan Fedotenko gets by Calgary's goalie, Miikka Kiprusoff. Vincent Lecavalier's pass set up the goal, Fedotenko's second of the game. DIRK SHADD/ST. PETERSBURG TIMES

Ruslan Fedotenko celebrates his first goal with Pavel Kubina. The Lightning won Game 7, 2-1, and took home the Stanley Cup. DIRK SHADD/ST. PETERSBURG TIMES

It is here because the Lightning won consecutive games for the first time in a series since Games 3 and 4 of the East semifinals and became the fifth team to win the Cup after falling behind three games to two in the finals.

It capped a thrilling season in which the team had a franchise-best 106 points, won a second straight Southeast title and was the No. 1 seed in the East. And the trophy is in the hands of captain Dave Andreychuk. The 40-year-old, in his 22nd season, won his first Cup in his first finals.

"Well, you dream about this day for a long time, obviously," he said. "I don't believe you can put into words the things that are going through your mind. I am going to savor this moment with my family and my teammates."

But still...

"Awesome," defenseman Dan Boyle said. "Everybody dreams about this when you are a kid. Nobody believed we were going to do it."

"The toughest loss by a thousand times," Flames wing Jarome Iginla said. "It hurts more than anything else I've been a part of to hear them out there celebrating."

It was sweet revenge for Fedotenko. Knocked out of Game 3 and out of Game 4 after being

With their 2-1 victory over the Flames on in Game 7 in front of a deafening, record St. Pete Times Forum crowd of 22,717, you saw the Lightning win the Stanley Cup.

"Unbelievable," wing Ruslan Fedotenko said. "I can't believe it. There are no words to express the feeling."

"Amazing," defenseman Jassen Cullimore said. "It's going to take a little time to set in. It's the Stanley Cup. It's in Tampa Bay."

pushed face-first by Robyn Regehr into the ledge of the boards, Fedotenko scored both goals, one in each of the first two periods. His 12 goals were just five fewer than he scored in the regular season.

Nikolai Khabibulin finished a postseason that likely assures he will be with the team next season. He made 16 saves and allowed only Craig Conroy's power-play goal through a screen 9:21 into the third. Cory Stillman and Vinny Lecavalier had assists as did Brad Richards, who, with 12 goals, a record seven winners and a playoff-high 26 points, got the Conn Smythe Trophy as playoff MVP.

"It's just last man standing," Richards said. "Basically, we might have won one more battle, gotten one more big save, another goal. One of those things that's unbelievable."

"It's overwhelming what they had to go through to get this," Lightning coach John Tortorella said. "I have nothing but respect for these athletes."

Scoring chances were at a premium. The teams, with 32 combined shots, broke the record for fewest in a Stanley Cup Finals game. That's why Stillman's work in the corner on Fedotenko's first goal was so invaluable.

Lecavalier's perfect pass, though surrounded by three defenders, set up Fedotenko's second goal. And Khabibulin was splendid in a third period in which Calgary took 10 of its 17 shots. His post-to-post save on Jordan Leopold with 4:55 left was a classic.

Martin St. Louis survived a cheap shot from Andrew Ference with 1:01 left. The blow into the boards cut his forehead, and Ference was called for boarding. And don't forget the effort from defensemen Pavel Kubina and Darryl Sydor, who helped hold Iginla, the likely MVP had the Flames won, to zero shots and without a point in consecutive games.

"We ran out of gas," Flames coach Darryl Sutter said. "We played as well as we could. But let's not forget, hey, we were beat by a great team."

The Lightning mob goaltender Nikolai Khabibulin after the final buzzer sounded, marking Tampa Bay's first-ever Stanley Cup. DIRK SHADD/ST. PETERSBURG TIMES

Lightning fans cheer with Ruslan Fedotenko after his first goal. DAN MCDUFFIE/ST. PETERSBURG TIMES

#19 BRAD RICHARDS

He always has been the "other guy."

When people talked about the Lightning, they talked about Vinny Lecavalier, you know, the No. 1 pick. They talked about Martin St. Louis. After all, he's probably going to win the league MVP this season.

Always the afterthought was Brad Richards, the little guy from the little province of Prince Edward Island. He wasn't the top pick. He isn't the league MVP. He isn't known as the star.

He never talked big. Or loud. Or often. That's not him.

What is he? Only the Conn Smythe winner for being the Most Valuable Player in the playoffs. With his parents—lobster fishermen in the Great White North—watching from the stands with tears in their eyes, commissioner Gary Bettman handed Richards the trophy after he was selected by the Professional Hockey Writers Association.

The little kid from PEI in the biggest hockey tournament in the world was the best player in the world.

"It doesn't matter where you are from," Richards said. "This is unbelievable."

As the playoffs progressed, Lightning players took turns being the star. Richards, though, was always the sidekick until he did it so often, he became the superhero of the postseason.

Richards showed up in every round.

In the first-round series against the Islanders, Richards had a goal and four assists in five games.

Height: 6'1"
Weight: 198
Position: C
Shoots: Left
Born: May 2, 1980
Montague, Prince
Edward Island

In the sweep of Montreal in the second round, Richards went back to where he played junior hockey and, along with old junior teammate Lecavalier, put on a show for his adopted hometown. He had three goals, including the overtime winner in Game 3, and an assist.

Then against the Flyers, Richards showed all his critics, the ones who hounded him since his days in junior hockey. Too soft, they said. They discounted his astounding offensive numbers in juniors because he played in the Quebec Major Junior Hockey League, considered the least physical of the three major junior leagues.

But against the rough-housing Flyers, Richards arrived. In seven grinding games full of bone-crunching hits, Richards scored four goals with four assists, including both helpers in a 2-1 Game 7 victory.

Then came the finals against the Flames, a team even more physical than the monsters from Philadelphia. He had an assist in Game 1, a goal and an assist in Game 2. He scored the only goal of Game 4. He picked up an assist in Game 5.

And in the do-or-die Game 6, Richards again showed the grit and heart many thought he didn't possess. He scored twice in the Lightning's 3-2 season-saving, double-overtime victory. In Game 7, Richards assisted on the crucial first goal, the goal that put Tampa Bay ahead to stay.

When the playoffs were over, Richards scored or assisted on 10 of the team's 16 game-winning goals. He finished with a team-high 12 goals and 14 assists. That made 26 points in 23 games.

That clutch performance earned him the trophy, barely over teammate Nikolai Khabibulin.

"I thought he was our best player," Khabibulin said. "He deserves to win it."

Now add Richards' name to the trophy previously won by legends such as Wayne Gretzky, Mario Lemieux and, Richards' idol, Joe Sakic.

"It's unbelieveable," Richards said. "I know it's a clichè, but you want to win the Cup. That's the goal and this [MVP] is the bonus. It's a great honor. It goes without saying." —TOM JONES

MVP Brad Richards is awarded the Conn Smythe Trophy.
BILL SERNE/ST. PETERSBURG TIMES

Pavel Kubina drinks from the Stanley Cup in the locker room. DIRK SHADD/ST. PETERSBURG TIMES

REGULAR-SEASON STATISTICS

Player	(Skaters)	Position	GP	G	A	PTS	+/-	PIM	ATOI	PPG	PPA	SHG	SHA	SOG	SPCT
26	Martin St. Louis	RW	82	38	56	94	35	24	20:34	8	22	8	3	212	17.9
61	Cory Stillman	LW	81	25	55	80	18	36	19:31	11	15	1	0	178	14.0
19	Brad Richards	C	82	26	53	79	14	12	20:25	5	21	1	1	244	10.7
4	Vincent Lecavalier	C	81	32	34	66	23	52	18:03	5	9	2	0	242	13.2
33	Fredrik Modin	LW	82	29	28	57	31	32	18:11	5	1	1	3	206	14.1
25	Dave Andreychuk	LW	82	21	18	39	-9	42	17:06	10	6	0	0	165	12.7
17	Ruslan Fedotenko	RW	77	17	22	39	14	30	14:38	0	1	0	0	116	14.7
22	Dan Boyle	D	78	9	30	39	23	60	22:45	3	12	0	0	137	6.6
13	Pavel Kubina	D	81	17	18	35	9	85	21:08	8	4	1	0	153	11.1
27	Tim Taylor	C	82	7	15	22	-5	25	12:53	0	0	0	2	95	7.4
37	Brad Lukowich	D	79	5	14	19	29	24	18:45	0	2	0	0	86	5.8
21	Cory Sarich	D	82	3	16	19	5	89	18:30	0	0	1	1	93	3.2
29	Dmitry Afanasenkov	LW	71	6	10	16	-4	12	12:20	0	2	0	0	98	6.1
7	Ben Clymer	RW	66	2	8	10	5	50	9:47	0	0	0	0	96	2.1
8	Martin Cibak	C	63	2	7	9	-1	30	7:35	0	0	0	0	44	4.5
5	Jassen Cullimore	D	79	2	5	7	8	58	19:01	0	0	0	0	78	2.6
55	Darryl Sydor	D	31	1	6	7	3	6	19:06	0	2	0	0	42	2.4
11	Chris Dingman	LW	74	1	5	6	-9	140	8:16	0	0	0	0	65	1.5
24	Shane Willis	RW	12	0	6	6	1	2	13:49	0	1	0	0	27	0.0
44	Nolan Pratt	D	58	1	3	4	11	42	16:25	0	0	0	1	35	2.9
36	Andre Roy	LW	33	1	1	2	-5	78	7:51	0	0	0	0	24	4.2
38	Darren Rumble	D	5	0	0	0	-2	2	11:33	0	0	0	0	5	0.0
9	Eric Perrin	C	4	0	0	0	-1	0	8:31	0	0	0	0	3	0.0

Player	(Goaltenders)	GP	W	L	T	GAA	TOI	SV	SV%	SHO	TGA	TSA	PIM	ENG
35	Nikolai Khabibulin	55	28	19	7	2.33	3273	1287	.910	3	127	1414	12	5
47	John Grahame	29	18	9	1	2.06	1688	606	.913	1	58	664	4	2

Acknowledgments

The entire staff of the *St. Petersburg Times* contributed to the coverage of the Tampa Bay Lightning's 2003-2004 championship season. In particular, we acknowledge the efforts of the sports, photography and research departments in compiling this commemorative book.

Sports Department

Assistant Sports Editor: Mike Stephenson

Columnists: Gary Shelton, John Romano

Writers: Damian Cristodero, Tom Jones, Joanne Korth, Brant James, Frank Pastor, Steve Lee, Emily Nipps

Designers: Jim Melvin, Christopher Cosenza

Copy Editors: Aaron Greenfield, Tim Sullivan, Jim Tomlin

Graphic Artist: Steve Madden

Photography Department

Photographers: Dirk Shadd and Dan McDuffie, Lightning Photo Team Leaders
Bill Serne, Doug Clifford, Stephen J. Coddington, Stefanie Boyar

Picture Editors: Sue Morrow, AME/Photography, Scott DeMuesy, Jack Rowland, Joe Walles

Photo Technology Director: Jack Rowland

Photo Technology Specialists: Georgina Brown, Donna Immerso, Richard Proplesch, Lynn Seelye, Tracee Stockwell, Jan Wilcox, Dan Workman, Steve Adolphson

News Library

Research Editor: John Martin
News Researcher: Cathy Wos

Marketing Department

Project Coordinator: Anthea Penrose

St. Petersburg Times

sptimes.com • tampabay.com